Cereb

DISABILITY, COUNSELLING /

CW00536325

BASIC TEXTS IN COUNSELLING AND PSYCHOTHERAPY

Series Editor: Stephen Frosh

This series introduces readers to the theory and practice of counselling and psychotherapy across a wide range of topic areas. The books will appeal to anyone wishing to use counselling and psychotherapeutic skills and will be particularly relevant to workers in health, education, social work and related settings. The books in this series are unusual in being rooted in psychodynamic and systemic ideas, yet being written at an accessible, readable and introductory level. Each text offers theoretical background and guidance for practice, with creative use of clinical examples.

Published

Jenny Altschuler
WORKING WITH CHRONIC ILLNESS

Bill Barnes, Sheila Ernst and Keith Hyde
AN INTRODUCTION TO GROUPWORK

Stephen Briggs
WORKING WITH ADOLESCENTS

Alex Coren
SHORT-TERM PSYCHOTHERAPY

Emilia Dowling and Gill Gorell Barnes
WORKING WITH CHILDREN AND PARENTS THROUGH SEPARATION AND DIVORCE

Gill Gorell Barnes
FAMILY THERAPY IN CHANGING TIMES

Ravi Rana
COUNSELLING STUDENTS

Paul Terry
COUNSELLING THE ELDERLY AND THEIR CARERS

Jan Wiener and Mannie Sher
COUNSELLING AND PSYCHOTHERAPY IN PRIMARY HEALTH CARE

Shula Wilson
DISABILITY, COUNSELLING AND PSYCHOTHERAPY

Invitation to authors

The Series Editor welcomes proposals for new books within the Basic Texts in Counselling and Psychotherapy series. These should be sent to Stephen Frosh at the School of Psychology, Birkbeck College, Malet Street, London, WC1E 7HX (email s.frosh@bbk.ac.uk).

Basic Texts in Counselling and Psychotherapy Series
Standing Order ISBN 0-333-69330-2
(outside North America only)

You can receive future titles in this series as they are published by placing a standing order. Please contact your bookseller or, in the case of difficulty, write to us at the address below with your name and address, the title of the series and the ISBN quoted above.

Customer Services Department, Macmillan Distribution Ltd.
Houndmills, Basingstoke, Hampshire RG21 6XS, England

DISABILITY, COUNSELLING AND PSYCHOTHERAPY

Challenges and Opportunities

SHULA WILSON

First published 2003 by
PALGRAVE MACMILLAN
Houndmills, Basingstoke, Hampshire RG21 6XS and
175 Fifth Avenue, New York, N.Y. 10010
Companies and representatives throughout the world

PALGRAVE MACMILLAN is the global academic imprint of the Palgrave Macmillan division of St. Martin's Press, LLC and of Palgrave Macmillan Ltd. Macmillan® is a registered trademark in the United States, United Kingdom and other countries. Palgrave is a registered trademark in the European Union and other countries.

ISBN 0–333–96496–9

This book is printed on paper suitable for recycling and made from fully managed and sustained forest sources.

A catalogue record for this book is available from the British Library.

Library of Congress Cataloging-in-Publication Data
Wilson, Shula, 1947–
    Disability, counselling, and psychotherapy: challenges and opportunities / Shula Wilson.
        p. cm. – (Basic texts in counselling and psychotherapy)
    Includes bibliographical references and index.
    ISBN 0–333–96496–9 (pbk.)
    1. People with disabilities – Mental health. 2. People with disabilities – Counselling of. I. Title. II. Series.

RC451.4.H35 W55 2002
362.4–dc21

                                                                                      2002028682

10 9 8 7 6 5 4 3 2 1
12 11 10 09 08 07 06 05 04 03

Printed and bound in Great Britain by
J. W. Arrowsmith Ltd, Bristol

CONTENTS

ACKNOWLEDGEMENTS

Through my work I have been privileged to meet many disabled people and their relatives who had the courage to share their fears, hopes and struggles. First and foremost I would like to thank these people, for I owe them the inspiration and many of the experiences that brought about this book. I am greatful to all the counsellors and psychotherapist who joined me at SKYLARK, dedicating their time and talent to work with people affected by disability.

I would also like to thank Dr Dorothy Judd for her clinical and literary guidance and encouragement, particularly her stimulating discussions and generous advice about the field of child psychotherapy. The interest shown by the women's book group provided ongoing and much needed support, and I especially thank Hilary Jarvis and Agatha Gwirts for their meticulous marking. My thanks also go to Dganit Iserlis and Angie Knorpel for their useful comments and critique.

Finally and most importantly I would like to thank my family for their patience and support while I was writing. Particular thanks go to Pete for his tireless proofreading, detailed editing and endless encouragement.

SHULA WILSON

To Adam and Amy

INTRODUCTION

Who is Disabled? What is Disability?

Disability is of concern to all of us as no one is immune to the loss of ability that can accompany an accident, illness or old age. No two people experience disability in the same way, just as no two people experience life in the same way.

For most disabled people their actual physical impairment is the least of their problems. A great deal of their frustration, hurt and pain results from the attitudes and reactions of other people to the impairment, ranging from denial and rejection to overcompensation. Some form of exclusion, or the wish to exclude, is a common reaction to disability. This book aims to demystify disability and argues that therapeutic work with disabled person should not be shrouded in mystery. Sensitive and competent therapists need to develop acute awareness and self-knowledge, and be able to monitor their own reactions to disability, both internal and external. Their main task, then, is to become aware of their own internal processes, including the conflict between attraction and repulsion that disability might evoke.

As a step towards developing such awareness we shall follow the stories of several disabled individuals from their therapist's perspective. These narratives are about the struggle to live a meaningful life beyond mere survival, to make sense of what seems unpredictable and chaotic and to find an autonomous place in the world.

The main theoretical ideas underpinning the clinical work have their roots in psychoanalysis. However to avoid unnecessary repetition the discussion will mainly be restricted to theoretical aspects that are specific to work with disabled people. I believe that this will enable the reader to integrate the understanding of disability and clinical practice presented in the text into his or her chosen approach to counselling and psychotherapy.

The object relations construct of disability, which has been developed through my work with disabled people, focuses on two main issues: the significance of the primary relationship between infant and caregiver, typically the mother–baby relationship: and awareness of human mortality, which leads to a variety of responses to death anxiety. The presence of disability at times acts as a reminder of death, thus creating a tension between the moral values of society and the survival instinct that drives us to eliminate the threat represented by human differences and imperfections.

The meaning and implications of the role therapists and other caregivers in their relationships with disabled people will be examined throughout the book. Amongst the questions to be addressed are:

■ What motivates a professional caregiver to choose this line of work?
■ What are the reactions to disability?
■ How does our own fear of disability and ultimately our fear of death affect the way we relate to disabled people?
■ What are the social and psychological motives for the tendency to deny disability and to reject and segregate disabled people?
■ What specialist knowledge, if any, is required for dealing with disabled people?

Chapter 1 discusses the social and cultural background to people's attitudes towards and reactions to disability. Among these is the concept of disability as a punishment, which stems from ancient myths. For example in Greek mythology the connection between scapegoat and punishment is well illustrated by the half-human, half-bull minotaur, who was viewed by his mother as a punishment for her infidelity. There is also a link between deformity and segregation as the mother creates the labyrinth to hide the minotaur, and thus hide the evidence of her sin (Graves, 1955, pp. 340–4). The experiences of today's disabled people suggest that these ancient perceptions and beliefs are still prevalent in current social attitudes.

Chapter 2 introduces the main ideas behind the development of the object relations construct of disability, or the relational model for short. Three models dominate the study of disability: the medical model, the social model and the analytical model. The medical model is about 'mending' disabled individuals so that they can function in the world of the non-disabled, the social model aims to 'mend' the non-disabled world so that it will embrace disabled people, and the analytical model is concerned with the internal experience of disability.

The relational model places the thinking and experiences of disabled people and those who work with them within a psychodynamic framework, as seen from an object relations perspective. The model is organised around the following elements: the individuation process, the formation of self-identity, and the struggle for autonomy experienced by disabled people. Developmental issues specific to the disabled infant are also explored, particularly the significance of the primary relationship between infant and caregiver, drawing on the thoughts of object relations theorists such as Klein (1932), Fairbairn (1952), Winnicott (1965b) and Mahler (1975). A distinction is made between people who are disabled from birth and those who acquire a disability later in life. The framework of adolescence as a the second stage of the individuation process and its four tasks, as described by Blos (1967), is utilised to illustrate the process in which autonomy can be regained and developed. Delays in the separation process are linked to difficulties with developing a clear sense of identity. This model also provides a useful tool for therapists to monitor their own reactions and thus enhance their awareness of the complexity of their interactions with disabled clients. The chapter ends with a vignette of the experience of a blind mother struggling for autonomy and dignity.

Chapter 3 addresses various aspects of managing the therapeutic relationship. The discussion consider why psychotherapists shy away from the issue of disability, both in clinical practice and as a theoretical consideration. Despite the growing interest in body–mind interactions and neuropsychology, the effects of disability on an adult's life receive very little attention. In the hope of increasing interest in work with disabled people and making it more 'therapist friendly', this chapter attends to the practical issues and emotional reactions that arise when working with disabled people. The therapist's role in restoring and encouraging the disabled client's autonomy is explored in a discussion about the first contact and assessment. The significance of third-party issues, external information, home visits, clients who need to be escorted and boundaries is highlighted by means of extensive case discussions. A fundamental element of the therapeutic interaction in general, and more so with disabled people, is the therapist's perception of the client as an autonomous individual. The complexity of working with clients whose physical dependency necessitates a high level of care and medical intervention is illustrated by a number of vignettes. The role of the therapist as the client's ally is compared and contrasted with that of other carers and health professionals.

When one is disabled the process of growing up, which is a difficult enough task for most people, is even more complicated. There are two main reasons for this. First the childhood experiences of disabled children are different from those of non-disabled children: because disabled children are restricted in their movement they are not free to explore and discover their own body and the world around them, to choose friends or to engage in physical activities. Second, uncertainty about the adult future awaiting children with a disability may cause great anxiety amongst primary caregivers, teachers and others who are involved in process of disabled children growing up.

In Chapter 4 Joe, a seven-year-old boy with cerebral palsy, takes us through the pain and joy of his struggle to face the world. When I first met Joe he reminded me of Don Quixote tilting at windmills. Like Cervantes' hero, Joe's perception of reality was somewhat distorted. Mixing fantasy with everyday reality was his way of defending himself against the painful harshness of being a disabled boy who was rejected by his father. The first breakthrough came when Joe asked 'What is disability?' and 'Why am I disabled?' He was asking for guidance in his effort to make sense of a world ridden with contradictions. Like many other children, Joe needed a safe place in which such questions could be asked and worked through. The relative freedom and autonomy he experienced in therapy helped to create an internal thinking space from which to face his internal and external worlds. The narrative also highlights the complex relationship between three agencies – home, school and therapy, all of which share the task of containing and holding the child.

The common experience of most young disabled adults is that others perceive them as immature, asexual, childlike beings. Chapter 5 discusses how Di, a young woman who was paralysed and unable to speak, and her therapist discovered a way to communicate, understand and respect each other with the help of a computer. Not being able to communicate means isolation and frustration. How can people with impaired speech project and assert their personality? The working assumption is that in the first instance attention needs to be given to the heightened anxiety experienced by the therapist as a result of the client's impaired speech. Without the habitual tool of language the therapist may feel anxious and unable to manage disturbing experiences. The therapist's experience is somewhat similar to that of an autistic person being bombarded with anxiety-provoking and unexplainable messages. This chapter also explores the effects of using an 'extension' – an external object that compensates for the non-functioning aspect of the body. Computer technology has added a new dimension to the way in which disabled people manage their environment and their relationships. For example it has enabled people who are able to hear and understand but are unable to speak to express themselves through an artificially produced voice or words on a screen.

The clinical discussion is organised around four phases of the therapeutic process:

- The referral procedure and pretherapy interactions.
- The process of building trust.
- Moving towards autonomy, consolidation and letting go.
- Making choices and taking risks.

The main theme of Di's story – 'I want someone who will love me' – paves the way to the next chapter and the discussion on sexuality and disability. For most people companionship, love and intimacy are an essential part of life. Chapter 6 discusses how disability, whether congenital or acquired, affects the way in which disabled and non-disabled people engage in their quest for love and intimacy. The experience of individuals is linked to their internal perspectives, including the developmental process and the significance of early relationships. The societal contexts in which individuals exist, including religion, social prejudices and everyday reactions to sex and disability, are carefully considered. Issues such as perversion, fear of deformity, attraction and disgust are discussed and illustrated with vignettes. The social pressure to distinguish between what is 'normal' and therefore acceptable, and what is not normal and therefore unacceptable, plays an important part in the disabled individuals formation of gender identity and sexual preferences. The chapter therefore includes disabled people's testimonies of how they experience their sexuality, all of which make clear that disabled people are sexual beings just like the rest of us.

Chapter 7 considers a controversial issue: The times when the struggle to survive is so exhausting that people look to a dignified end rather than prolonged humiliation. Perhaps there is a stage when the struggle with physical and emotional pain combine with institutionalisation to render life not worth fighting for, especially when the individuals concerned feel that society has already cast them out. Ron, whose story unfolds in this chapter, had never been able to separate himself from his mother. At the age of 40, soon after his mother died, he developed a fear of walking that had no neurological explanation. Margaret Mahler, in her case study of 15-month-old Teddy, describes the tension between the physical ability to walk and the fear of letting go. The interplay between the toddler's conflict and the mother's anxiety prevented the development of the autonomous function of walking (Mahler *et al.*, 1975). Both Teddy and Ron had the physical ability to walk but lacked the emotional ability to let go. For Ron it seems that the death of his mother took him back to the toddler stage and he could not progress without her. The therapeutic relationships discussed in this book, offer a useful guideline for negotiating ways of holding on to responsibilities and letting go of fears. Those therapists who are willing and able to work with disabled people often experience a strong force that pushes them beyond the boundaries of the therapeutic frame. Through the clinical discussions it is demonstrated how clients and therapists deal with the temptation to break the rules when anxiety becomes unmanageable and go on to develop productive ways of facing reality.

A note regarding clinical material

The clinical material in this book is intended to help practitioners who are interested in working with disabled people to develop an awareness of their own reactions to disability, as well as an understanding of the perception and experiences of disabled people.

The term 'client', rather than 'patient', is used to differentiate psychotherapy from medical treatment. While the terms 'counsellor', 'psychotherapist' and 'therapist' are interchangeable the use of 'counsellor' is avoided due to its wider applications, such as 'debt counsellor' or youth guides in the American context.

Finally, while the identity of all the characters in this book has been disguised their experiences are real.

1

CULTURAL, SOCIAL AND PERSONAL ASPECTS OF DISABILITY

A Disabled Person's Experience

Anne McDonald was born with cerebral palsy. She was placed in a hospital at the age of three and remained until her eighteenth birthday, locked into a hospital regime that might have led to her death. In the preface to her book, *Annie's Coming Out* she writes:

> To be imprisoned inside one's own body is dreadful. To be confined to an institution for the profoundly retarded does not crush you in the same way; it just removes all hope.
>
> I went to St Nicholas Hospital when I was three. The hospital was the state garbage bin. Very young children were taken into permanent care, regardless of their intelligence. If they were disfigured, distorted or disturbed then the world should not have to see or acknowledge them. You knew that you have failed to measure up to the standard expected of babies. You were expected to die.
>
> Never seeing normal children, we were not sure what they were like. Where did we fall short? In your ugly body it was totally impossible that there could be a mind. Vital signs showed that your title was 'human'; but this did not entitle you to live like normal children. You were totally outside the boundary which delineated the human race. (Crossley and McDonald, 1984)

In this short extract Anne McDonald summarises her experience at the receiving end of the social rejection and segregation mechanism. The tactic was to dehumanise those who were different and therefore failed to measure up. The aim of this dehumanisation was to enable society to rid itself of guilt and to provide a moral justification for discarding 'rejects' by removing them from human society and eventually from life.

Rosemary Crossley, the teacher who together with Anne MacDonald wrote *Annie's Coming Out*, quotes Annie's relatives' reactions when they first saw her:

> 'Well, if it was a puppy you'd knock it on the head, wouldn't you?' one of them said. Another was not only tactless but also senile and deaf and kept repeating loudly like a cracked record, 'If it was my child I'd kill it and you could not blame me.' (Ibid., pp. 82–3)

The wish to annihilate the deformed or bad object is expressed here in two ways. The more 'civilised' person needed to dehumanise the disabled person by likening her to a puppy before imagining the killing. The senile person, who had lost the thin veneer of civilisation, was able to envisage killing a human being but still had some fear of being blamed and punished for it.

In this chapter and throughout the book I shall argue that the experience of disability is less about impairment and more about the reactions of those within the disabled person's social environment, including parents, family, professional carers (psychotherapists included) and society at large

LEARNING POINT

- Disabled people and their carers are often confronted with the unconscious or conscious desire of non-disabled people to eliminate disability, often by dehumanising the disabled person.

Privacy, Dignity and the Tendency to Infantilise Disabled People

The first step towards dehumanising people is to strip them of their privacy and dignity. Most of the authors who have written about their own disability (for example Begum, 1996; Brown, 1954; Keith, 1994, 2000; Morris, 1996; Murphy, 1987; Oliver, 1996; Shakespeare, 1998; Williams, 1994) and those who have written about them (for example Erskin and Judd, 1994; Jureidini, 1988; Lussier, 1960, 1980; Taylor, 1987) seem to agree on one elementary point: that the major cause of emotional distress for disabled people is not the actual physical impairment, but the effect that the impairment has on their relationship with others and their ability to manage the environment. Donna Williams

2

(1994, p. 195) relating her experience as an autistic young woman, says 'allowing me my privacy and space was the most beneficial thing I ever got. Only the unthreatening nature of privacy and safety would inspire the courage to explore the world, step by step.'

Those of us who have ever been ill or injured would agree that the most noticeable changes that take place are loss of privacy and the removal of responsibility for one's own body. Doctors, nurses, carers and a variety of therapists take over the intimate and private task of attending to one's bodily needs and functions, and the experience of being a hospital patient is frequently associated with loss of dignity. For a non-disabled person, hospitalisation is a time-limited experience and the pain and humiliation involved are tolerated as a necessary part of treatment that will lead to recovery. For the great majority of disabled people, however, the condition that earned them the label 'disabled' does not include recovery in its prognosis. The pain and humiliation that non-disabled people associate with short-term hospitalisation can be a life-long companion for disabled people.

A common childhood memory shared by many Western adults concerns the way in which some parents and other carers disregard children's privacy. The human infant is entirely dependent on being looked after by an 'other', that is, the mother or her substitute. The task of looking after allows the carer free access to the infant's body and space. At this stage total lack of privacy is necessary to the survival of the infant, and as long as the degree to which the infant's freedom is interfered with matches its real needs the invasion will be experienced as appropriate and welcome by the infant. Yet the adult carer is rarely able fully to appreciate the infant's needs. This might be due to communication difficulties, child-rearing traditions or the carer's own personal history. The gap between the infant's perceived needs and the adult's perception of these needs often leads to over- or under-care. Over-care is characterised by unnecessary restrictions on the infant's freedom, under-care by the reverse, perhaps to the point of neglect.

Most of us, whether disabled or not, experienced both over-care and under-care to some degree during our years of childhood dependency. For non-disabled adults this experience belongs to the past, but many disabled adults are not so lucky – despite reaching adulthood they are still unable to care fully for themselves and may have to be depend on people other than themselves in order to survive and function. This carer–client dyad is formed as a response to the constraints of disability. Although different from the mother – baby dyad, it nonetheless echoes a variety of childhood experiences for both the carer and the person being cared for. Some disabled people have to be looked after in a way that is reminiscent of looking after a baby: they have to be fed, washed and dressed. *Yet they are not babies.*

We all accept that a baby cannot make decisions because its experience and ability to process knowledge are insufficient for the task. Therefore it is accepted that the mother/carer should have access to as much information as possible about the baby so that she can make well-informeded decisions on its behalf. For this reason it seems appropriate and acceptable that the baby is completely stripped of privacy. At times the mother has to handle the baby's body against its wishes, the nurse has to measure or inject and the doctor pokes into orifices. Everything is done for 'the baby's own good'. For many disabled people this does not stop at infancy because they are perceived as eternal infants or 'unfinished' adolescents. Both disabled adults and their carers are engaged in an ongoing struggle to understand and make sense of what it means to be disabled. How can an impaired body support a fully functioning, mature mind?

LEARNING POINT

■ The dignity and privacy afforded a disabled person can be influenced by the confusion caused when an adult person needs infant care. The attitudes and perceptions of disabled people and their carers become confused.

The Social Context of the Disabled Child

How we relate to disability depends on our personal history, the experiences and relationships we have had and the traditions and values we hold.

Winnicott's innovative contribution to psychoanalysis is the concept of the mother–infant unit: 'the centre of gravity of the being does not start off in the individual. It is in the total set up' (Winnicott, 1975, p. 99). The saying 'There is no such thing as a baby, only a mother and a baby' focuses not on the baby as an independent entity but on the mother–baby dyad. Behind this concept lies the basic fact that the baby's chance of survival depends on the maternal figure's ability and willingness to hold and nurture this helpless being, rather as a baby kangaroo is held in its mother's pouch. But what happens when a baby is born disabled, or becomes disabled in infancy? What effect will this have on the mother's holding and nurturing? What is the adaptive component necessary for the survival and the well-being of the mother–baby dyad? Reactions to the birth of a physically impaired baby reflect the diversity of human reactions to the unpredictable. We shall look at these reactions from the general cultural perspective and from the individual's own experience.

A mother's culture, social group and belief system intermingle to determine the way in which she and those in her social environment respond to the fact that she has given birth to a baby that is different from the one they all had wished for. Her ability to value and respect herself could be affected by the birth of an 'impaired' child. During pregnancy she imagines and relates to her unborn child as though it is normal – compatible with her group's (family's/community's) perception of the ideal member of the group. The arrival of a baby who is different, and therefore does not conform to the ideal, acts as an unwelcome reminder of the limited control we have over even a personal process such as pregnancy. This sense of helplessness brings with it fear, anxiety and a need to regain control in the face of failed predictability.

Culture of cause and effect

The birth of an impaired child, an injury that results in impairment and the diagnosis of a chronic or terminal illness are often referred to as a tragedy. The notion of tragedy implies both drama and disaster. The tragic event disturbs the established order and offers the threat of a chaotic world in which anything could happen to anyone. For most of us the possibility of an unpredictable and chaotic world is too frightening to contemplate. As a defence against this fear, individuals and groups attempt to maintain a sense of control by devising an explanation whereby the tragic event is perceived as a deviation from the norm, from stability and predictability. In many cultures and belief systems this explanation is based on the 'crime and punishment' principle. Cultures differ in the way in which the sinner is identified and how the punishment is inflicted. For example Christianity postulates that the original sin was committed by Eve, the mythological maternal figure, the mother of all beings who was seduced by the serpent to eat the forbidden fruit of the tree of knowledge, and in turn seduced Adam to eat with her. This disobedience had to be atoned for by Adam and Eve's descendents: 'The successful sinner would be punished in his descendant' (Dodds, 1951, p. 33). In the Old Testament the prophets Jeremiah and Ezekiel repeat the same warning: 'In those days they shall say no more, The fathers have eaten a sour grape, and the children's teeth are set on edge, one shall die for his own iniquity' (Jeremiah, 31:29), and 'What mean ye, that ye use this proverb saying The fathers have eaten sour grapes, and the children's teeth are set on edge? The soul that sinneth, it shall die' (Ezekiel, 18:2,4). While maintaining their belief in punishment for crime the two prophets contest the popular perception that the sinner can avoid penalty by passing on the punishment to his descendants.

In analytical terms the idea expressed in the proverb could also be seen as a defence against guilt and shame. When society and/or parents are unable to contain what is experienced as unbearable guilt for failing to prevent a baby's impairment while at the same time feeling shame for wanting to get rid of the impaired child, a defence mechanism operates by projecting what is perceived as the bad object onto an external body, which ironically in this case is the very same child.

In Western thinking the term 'culture of guilt' refers to the moral aspect of cause and effect: 'When we call one object, *Cause*; the other, *Effect*, we suppose that there is some connection between them; some power in the one, by which it infallibly produces the other, and operates with the greatest certainty and strongest necessity' (Hume, 1977, p. 75). The Bible and Greek mythology strongly influenced this questionable way of making sense of the world. For example the legend of the minotaur illustrates how the ancient Greeks saw the connection between sin and punishment. In Greek mythology Parsiphae gave birth to the minotaur, which was half human and half bull. She was ashamed of its beastly nature and felt guilty as she believed that her infidelity to her husband, King Minos, had caused the birth of this half beast. In order to hide what she thought was evidence of her sin she commissioned the architect Daedalus to construct a labyrinth from which the minotaur could not escape, and into which no one could enter from outside. This exemplifies the use of segregation to hide what makes us feel guilty.

A deed can become a sin if it is a morally or socially condemned act, as in Parsiphae's infidelity, or it can be an otherwise non-sinful event invested with sin. As the mother of a severely disabled child once said to me, 'I have enjoyed myself too much, so this is how I pay for it.' The need to make sense of her world and find an explanation brought this mother to equate 'enjoying life' with sin. She could not accept the possibility of randomness, and in order to maintain her belief in a just system she had to find a cause for her child's condition and to define it as a sin. In the West the strong propensity for scientific thinking creates an expectation for all occurrences to have a reason, to be the result of a known or identifiable cause, and to make sense.

It is important, however, to remember that the idea of a link between the disabled child and the mother's (or father's) supposed wrongdoings is not a universal one. In non-Western cultures where there is a belief in reincarnation or life after death, disability is not necessarily regarded as a negative or a permanent condition, and impairment is seen as resulting from an event in the disabled person's previous life, not the mother's current life. For example Reiter *et al.* (1986, p. 359) state that the Druse sect in the Middle East regard disability as 'a temporary or passing condition', with the possibility of change ocurring in life after death. Likewise Leonard's (1985) report on disability in Sri Lanka and Edgerton's (1981) review of attitudes towards children with learning disabilities in parts of India both support the view that among cultural groups that believe in reincarnation, disability is perceived as a temporary condition that affects just one of many lives.

While many belief systems attempt to make sense of disability by assuming causality they differ significantly in respect of the role of the mother. In the West there is a tendency to view a child's disability as the mother's responsibility or even her fault, while in many non-Western cultures the child is viewed as a separate individual who is responsible for his or her own fate. In the East the belief in reincarnation may account for parents' less traumatic adjustment to their infant's disability, and in some instances the parents of a disabled child may see themselves as especially chosen for this important role.

LEARNING POINTS

- The need to explain the inexplicable as a means of maintaining a sense of control over one's own fate is common to most cultures.
- Regardless of the specific cultural context, the phenomenon of impairment poses a threat to the desired order, to normality.
- The cause and effect explanation is often used as a defence, which works as follows: The impairment, injury or illness is seen as a disaster that can strike again. A cause has to be identified so that individuals or the group can find a way to prevent such disasters in the future.
- In most cases disability is unpredictable, unexpected and mostly unwanted. Having a disabled child can undermine the parents' sense of security, which is based on the known and expected order of things.
- Looking for an explanation is an attempt to restore the belief that there is a reliable order. Blaming the mother for her child's fate offers one such explanation.

Attitudes and reactions to body differences

Why are difference and imperfection so disturbing? Let us first look at the effect on the individual. Take for example the strange phenomenon of the phantom limb – an arm or a leg that lingers indefinitely in the mind of the person long after it is lost. What is it that interferes with the process of accepting and adjusting to changes in the body? Most of us share an image of the body as a whole. In a discussion about phantom limbs Merleau-Ponty (1962, p. 82), the French philosopher, suggests that 'our body comprises as it were two distinct layers, that of the habit-body and that of the body at this moment'. The 'habit body' is also the expected body. In the phantom limb syndrome the mind refuses to accept the 'body at this moment' – the body without a limb – and is holding on to the wished-for body, imagining that all the limbs are still in place. As most individuals share the concept of the whole body the phantom limb syndrome – the refusal to accept that a part of one's body is missing or damaged – could be extended to explain some parents' refusal to accept their impaired child. When parents overidentify and perceive their child as an extension of their own bodies, the impairment to the child's body may seem like an impairment to their own, which they are unable to accept. For such parents, dehumanisation of the child is their way of facilitating separation.

Weiss (1997) notes that in Israel some parents tend to isolate their disabled children from the family territory and the child is defined as a non-person. That is, the parents and perhaps other members of the community relate to the impaired child as though he or she is an object or belongs to a different species. The quality of the 'caging' in which the impaired child is housed can vary from a tumbledown shed in the back yard to a nicely decorated nursery under lock and key at the far end of the house. In Weiss's study parents' reaction to their impaired child is presented as one step removed from active physical elimination: 'I don't want her to cross my threshold. This is like a creature from outer space. Like a devil' (Ibid., p. 265). These are the words with which a father welcomed his newborn daughter. In another case a mother (who was a psychotherapist) described her two-year-old daughter, who was locked away in a separate annex of the house and did not mix with her siblings, as follows: 'She isn't like us. She's like a little animal. She can't live with us' (Ibid., p. 267). Likening a disabled child to the devil or an animal can be interpreted as the parents' justification for their wish to be rid of their impaired, unwanted child. Dehumanising is a way of separating 'us' (humans) from 'them' (non-humans – devil or animal). Giving birth to an impaired child is taken as indicating an impairment the parents, in which case denying the humanity of the child and regarding him or her as 'not one of us' severs the link between the child and the parents and thus the link with the impairment.

The parents in Weiss's study tried to arrange for their impaired children to be put into institutions, but failing this they created an institution within the home. Weiss found that some of the parents viewed their child's impairment as an awful mistake for which somebody other than themselves should take responsibility. The maternal instinct does not seem to have been in operation here. – the children were openly rejected by their mothers. The parents were not able to cope, and their wish for the future was that the disabled child would somehow disappear, like a bad dream. Fortunately this reaction is not so prevalent. For example Affleck *et al.* (1985) have found that mothers who see themselves as responsible for their child's disability seem to cope well with the child's needs, perhaps because they manage to identify a reason for their child's impairment and thus their sense of control stays intact.

LEARNING POINTS

- By attempting to clear away the different, 'damaged' child, the family is endeavouring to maintain its self-image as normal, whole and perfect.
- Another reason why the child is hidden away is that its physical presence is a painful reminder of the guilt felt for 'allowing' the impairment and shame for wishing to annihilate it. To alleviate this guilt and shame the child has to be dehumanised and pushed out of sight.
- Paradoxically, parents who accept responsibility for their child's disability are often effective and affectionate.

Institutions and Institutionalisation

Institutions as a defence against the fear of difference and death anxiety

Based on a pilot study of residential institutions Miller and Gwynne (1972, p. 80) summed up the role of institutions for disabled people: 'The task that society assigns – behaviourally though never verbally – to these institutions is to cater for the socially dead during the interval between social death and physical death.' The guilt and shame embedded in keeping disabled people separated from the non-disabled could also be related to death anxiety: their apparent helplessness acts as a reminder of the death awaiting us all. Thus our wish to deny our vulnerability by eliminating reminders of it can lead to acts of aggression such as locking people away, which is then justified as an act of self-preservation. Freud considered that aggression derives from the death instinct being redirected against the external world: 'The instinct of distraction, moderated and tamed, and as it were, inhibited in its aim, must, when it is directed toward objects, provide the ego with the satisfaction of its vital needs and with control over nature' (Freud, 1961, vol. 21, p. 121).

The instinct behind the need to seek control over nature is probably a powerful motivator of the way in which institutions are managed. There is an innate dichotomy here: institutions are there to offer care and support to the helpless, and at the same time to protect the rest of society from the helpless.

LEARNING POINTS

■ If one accepts that society needs to be protected from the helpless, then it follows that helplessness is threatening and should be annihilated or at least hidden away.
■ The power and authority vested in institutions can easily be abused or misused.

Positive institutions

An attempt to create a positive institution is reported by Dartington et al. (1981). They studied the first year of operation of a residential unit for people with disabilities and found a failure to bring about the declared intention to create an environment in which the residents could control their own lives and reality:

> The assumption that disabled people have choices in their lives and with help can have autonomous personalities, separate from the personalities of those on whom they are physically dependent, has not yet been fully realised because ultimately the able-bodied retain authority for defining the reality within which the disabled are free to live. (Ibid., 1992a p. 65, 71)

It seems that those who set up this positive institution were caught in a conflict between the conscious desire to create an environment in which disabled people would have freedom of choice as autonomous beings, and the archaic, unconscious need to defend themselves against the anxiety and sense of helplessness evoked by the presence of disability

Bion's (1961) concept of 'basic assumption group', which meets in order to be sustained by a leader upon whom it depends for material or spiritual nourishment and protection, is useful for explaining one aspect of the institutionalisation process. In the past this leader took the form of God, but now the state and its agencies are expected to look after us. Thus in the creation of institutions such as hospitals, residential homes and day centres there is an element of society's attempt to replicate the role of Bion's omnipotent leader. The magical power invested in institutions as the main solution to human suffering prompts a denial of the poor quality of life in and a prolonging of the suffering caused by the very same institutions. Institutionalisation, which means handing over control and giving up autonomy, perpetuates and increases the need for help, thus ensuring that help is consistently needed from the institution, which is seen as the external, all-powerful controlling source (Menzies-Lyth, 1988). In recent years there has been a strong and on the whole positive move away from institutionalisation and back into the community, but the community, as shown in Weiss's (1997) study, is not always prepared or willing to include those who are different.

LEARNING POINT

■ Institutions and institutionalisation are major part of the life of many disabled people, while at the sametime serving to remove the anxieties of non-disabled people.

On Becoming a Professional Caregiver

The Shorter Oxford English Dictionary defines 'institution' as 'The appointment of a person in cure of souls' and 'an established practice'. Thus the caring profession as a whole can be described as an institution, and counselling and psychotherapy are part of that institution. Against this backdrop a fundamental question has to be asked: what is it that attracts caregivers in general, and psychotherapists in particular to their occupation? Langs, who pioneered the communicative approach to psychotherapy, suggested a poignant answer: the 'universal need for idols and revered paternal figures whose omnipotence and omniscience help to support a similar universal need to deny all sense of personal vulnerability and mortality' (Langs, 1992a, p. 15). Therapists and other caregivers may be unconsciously seeking a position that gives them the power to control others, which can be seen as a way of denying their own fears and hence the risk of unconsciously abusing this power is always lurking in the background (Guggenbühl-Craig, 1971; Marmor, 1953)

The fantasy of defeating death by becoming a healer may, paradoxically, bring therapists into a situation in which the psychological factors and emotional experiences of death are an ever-present and powerful manifestation of latent issues. Therapist' may then be tempted to deny their own weakness by adopting a theory or practice that construes the client as the weak party in the dyad and the therapist as the strong one, thus denying the possibility of gaining insights into their respective inner realities. The temptation to assume power and control increases in direct proportion to the intensity of the presence of the death-related element, such as when doctors seek legal support for a medical intervention aimed at defeating death against the patient's expressed wish. Therefore as a death-reminding element, Physical disability is likely to add weight to the seductiveness of omnipotence. The relative absence of psychoanalytical writing on the subject of death and a similar lack on the subject of disability suggests a link between disability and death anxiety that manifested in the avoidance of disability as a representation of the fragility of physical existence. Therefore therapists who want to work with disabled people must resolve of their own death anxiety and recognise their tendency to use defences, particularly denial.

An occupational hazard – misuse of power as a defence against anxiety

While we know that impairment is not contagious we are aware that we could become impaired – we know that an accident or an illness can strike at any moment. How does the psyche cope with the fear of loss, pain and suffering associated with impairment? The coping mechanisms are set on a continuum stretching from defences against the fear and anything that might trigger it, to the endeavour to understand and accept impairment as an integral part of the human condition. Most of us oscillate between these two polarities. Professional carers, including therapists, run a high risk of overusing their professional defences.

Interpreting the meaning of help and care

June's rheumatoid arthritis was characterised by flare-ups that caused great pain and paralysis. After few months in therapy she talked of her experience with a non-disabled therapist:

> Once when I was in therapy with a woman I respected very much, she read me an article with great enthusiasm about a diet which purportedly can cure rheumatoid arthritis. She looked up when she finished reading and I was crying. 'How could you?' I said. She had become like everyone else. It was as if she stopped seeing me and only saw my medical condition.

Why was June so distressed? After all the therapist was trying to be helpful – or was she? In June's mind the therapist's action had turned her from a special person into just another professional who was imposing her own agenda rather than listening. The fact that the article was read to her suggested to June that the therapist perceived her as not doing enough to look after herself, and as not intelligent enough to comprehend the medical world. June felt that by suggesting a cure, her therapist was saying that she would never be all right as long as she was disabled, and that taking better care of herself would solve the problem. Although not consciously intended by the therapist, this humiliating message instilled in June a sense of guilt for contracting the disease and shame for not treating it properly. She felt infantilised and excluded.

Why did a therapist who had been respected by her client, resort to such behaviour? To answer this question, let us look at the individual elements of the story:

- The therapeutic relationship had been going on for some time.
- The client had rheumatoid arthritis.
- Reading the article was uncharacteristic behaviour for the therapist.
- The client was deeply hurt and upset

We can safely assume that the therapist did not consciously intend to upset her client. But the client's disability acted as an unconscious reminder of the therapist's own vulnerability, and caused her to feel stuck, hopeless and helpless. The possibility of developing rheumatoid arthritis and the knowledge that there was nothing to immunise her against it was more than she could face at the time. She needed a break, a respite. By reading the article she removed herself from the reality of her client into the realm of science and professional control, leaving her client behind. As is so often the case with professionals who work with disabled people, she was unconsciously attempting to defend herself against the helplessness evoked by the presence of disability, against the threat of becoming disabled. She could no longer contain the anxiety triggered by the client's condition and needed to create a barrier between herself and her client. Reading the article offered her momentary relief from her fear, but at what cost! Unless a therapist is able to recognise, acknowledge and work through untherapeutic conduct with the client she will no longer be of help to her client. If the deviation is not adressed the client will not be able to trust the therapist's ability to address her own anxieties let alone her client's.

Behind the benevolent and seemingly generous act of giving may sometimes lie the wish to separate, through disguised ways of patronising and infantilising the client. It is very tempting to relate to a disabled person as one would to an infant. To remain a professional helper one needs to ask oneself, what do I mean by helping? Let us look at a clichéd but illustrative scenario. A blind man was standing by a crossing. He seemed a little agitated and restless. A sighted women passing by spotted him, grabbed hold of his arm and while marching him across the road said 'Don't worry dear, I'll help you to get to the other side'. As it happened the blind man was standing by the rail waiting for a friend who had been delayed, hence the agitation. He had not wanted to cross the road. This situation is an everyday occurrence for many disabled people, who in this over-care scenario are viewed and treated at best as infants and at worst as objects. The do-gooder made two assumptions: that the blind man wanted to cross the road, and that he would need/want her help. She could have confirmed her assumptions by asking a simple question, such as 'Do you need any help?' Would she have behaved the same way towards a person she regarded as her equal? The act of disrespecting the private space and dignity of the other is a form of defence disguised as a good intention, and is frequently used in relation to disabled people.

LEARNING POINTS

- Impairment, whether existing from birth or acquired later in life, is unexpected, 'out of order' and 'not according to plan', thus its presence disturbs the order upon which the belief system that explains and makes sense of the world is based.
- For a non-disabled person the existence of a person who is different in shape and the way in which she or he functions can be experienced as a threat as it suggests that one's own body might become deformed or malfunctional.

IMPLICATIONS FOR THERAPISTS

- Recognising our own vulnerability is the first step towards letting go of the defences that could prevent us from tolerating our client's fears, helplessness and hopelessness. This is not specific to disability but applies to all therapeutic and care work, although disability tends to make concret and intensify anxiety and reactions.
- The need to defend themselves against the threat of chaos posed by disability could impair the effectiveness of therapists and other professionals. Moreover there is a risk that therapists who cannot contain their pain, frustration and anxiety will inadvertently project these emotions onto their clients.
- The irrational fear that disability is infectious never ceases to scare.
- When therapists become aware of an urge to deviate and introduce irrelevant and inappropriate activities they should stop and ask themselves why, what it is that is going on subconsciously. The activiy of psychotherapy consists of listening to clients and trying to make sense of their world.

Autonomy: the Story of Mary

Mary's story illustrates one aspect of the difficulties faced by a disabled people who try to maintain their dignity and privacy. Mary was in her mid thirties and led an active life, attending to her responsibilities as a single mother to her 13-year-old daughter Gill and holding down a full-time job. Mary was blind, but her guide dog allowed her to retain her freedom of movement. She sought therapy at a local-authority-supported free counselling service specialising in disability because she was very distressed about Gill's education and her own role as a single blind mother. Gill's schoolwork and behaviour were deteriorating – she was mixing with a group of youngsters who Mary felt were having a bad influence on her. In desperation Mary asked for help at her church. The priest thought that the best solution would be to send Gill to a boarding school. Mary agreed as it seemed a good idea at the time. The church's congregation provided the necessary money and arranged for a school placement. Soon after Gill went away Mary felt that she had made the wrong decision. She thought that for Gill it was much too early to be leaving home and that she herself was not yet ready to part from her child. She was thinking of bringing Gill back home but the priest and the others involved did not approve of her change of mind.

One day Mary arrived for her therapy session in a very agitated state. On the way from the main door to the consulting room she said, 'These people here, you can't trust them, they put some barricades in the way; the dog could not find a way round them, luckily this person passed by and helped us.' During the session Mary spoke about a letter she had received from the priest, accusing her of being selfish and ignoring her daughter's needs. She was very angry and said, 'Why did he have to send me a letter? He knows somebody will have to read it for me. He could have put it on a tape if he had had any consideration for me. I lost all my privacy, other people know about my personal affairs before I do!'

The theme running through these two comments was Mary's frustration and inability to control her own affairs due to environmental impingements (barricades, the priest's letter), which led to exposure and loss of privacy (having to ask for help). The barricades on the way to the therapy session may have symbolised for Mary the therapist's inability to create a therapeutic space free of obstacles where she could come and go without being noticed. She had welcomed the help offered by the therapist, but the fact that she needed to be helped was a painful reminder of the limited control she had over her own affairs. Mary had had to expose herself to the person who lad helped her on the way to therapy and to the friend who had read the priest's letter to her. The implicit message in the letter was that Mary was acting irresponsibly, that she could not be a good mother to her child because she could not see. This disrespectful and infantilising message had been read aloud by her friend – her humiliation had been made public. For Mary, living in the world of sighted people meant that she had to tolerate considerable humiliation and exposure due to sighted people's lack of consideration.

During the interpretation the therapist suggested a link between the priest's power as representative of the church and what could be perceived as the therapist's power as an 'authority'. Another link was between the power that the people at church assumed over her by paying the school fees, and the fact that she was not paying for her therapy. Receiving therapy free of charge could have been an echo of the experience of being patronised by the church. Using therapy to work through her disturbing relationship with the church authority enabled Mary to question and reassess the power she had invested in others and reclaim her autonomy by bringing Gill back home.

Winnicott's (1988) concept of impingement provides a useful way of understanding the process by which autonomy is undermined in a dependency relationship where there is an overt or covert power imbalance. The term impingement, according to Winnicott, covers two aspects of maternal failure. The first is excessive maternal attention, or over-care. A worried mother who is unsure of herself relieves her anxiety about her overwhelming responsibility for her child by keeping herself constantly engaged in activities relating to the infant. This over-activity disturbs the infant as it interferes with the process of adjustment to and integration into the world. Winnicott points out that when babies are in a relaxed state they are actually engaged in the process of coming out of their original state of formlessness and unintegration, and therefore should not be disturbed.

The second aspect of maternal failure is lack of attention or passivity. This occurs when the mother is too preoccupied with her own affairs to pick up the baby's cues or provide an appropriate response to the hallucinatory creations and needs of the infant when he or she is in an excited or active state.

Both kinds of maternal deficiency, which I referred to earlier as over-care and under care, are experienced by the infant as 'an interruption of being' (Winnicott, 1988, p. 127). Ideally a caregiver should be able both to hold the baby's formlessness and to provide the stimulation that is necessary for growth. Any interference with these functions is experienced by the infant as an impingement; that is, the 'outside' is making demands rather than responding. The carer's role is twofold: to allow the infant 'continuity of being' by respecting its need for solitude, and to respond to its opposite need for play and stimulation.

Having to respond to impingement distracts the infant from its own life process and forces it to react to unpredictable external demands. As a way of defending itself against such impingements the infant develops what Winnicott calls the 'false self': a persona that acts as a barrier between the true self and the outside world.

Impingement does not end with infancy: adults in dependency relationships can also experience it. Mary's story illustrates the dynamic of impingement in respect of dependency relationships. Mary perceived herself as not good enough to mother Gill and therefore sought outside help, perhaps a substitute partner/father. Because she felt inadequate as a blind mother she transferred her autonomy and power to the priest. A sense of helplessness is characteristic both of Mary's perception of herself as an inadequate mother and of the infant's experience of being an incomplete and inadequate human being. Mary believed that a strong parental figure such as the church was needed. The church, however, interpreted her plea for help as an invitation to take over. Thus instead of listening the powerfull party assumes full knowledge of and control over the dependant's needs and acts upon this assumption. The same could be said of the mother who assumes she knows what her child needs without actually checking with the child.

LEARNING POINTS

■ The desire to exert power and control over others, mainly those who appear weak, is a common human trait. In the caring professions the exercise of authority carries with it the hazard of creating a feeling of superiority in the authority figure.

■ Holding on to authority for its own sake is psychologically unhealthy for those who dominate and those who are dominated.

■ The need for deference could indicate underlying anxiety and insecurity.

■ One way of safeguarding against the misuse of power is to work towards a democratic interpersonal relationship.

Summary

This chapter has introduced the predicaments experienced by disabled people in their cultures, social groups and families. Institutions and institutionalisation have also been discussed, with attention to their role as a barrier to the anxiety provoked by the presence of disability. The chapter ended with the story of Mary to illustrate the relational issues that confront disabled people, particularly the way in which autonomy and dignity are impinged upon.

A diversity of approaches and an apparent lack of universality seem to emerge from this brief overview of some of the cultural and social factors that influence people's attitudes towards disability. Disability, like beauty, is a relative rather than an absolute concept. The therapeutic tools that need to be sharpened are therapists' awareness of their own internal processes and careful attention to their clients' conscious and unconscious communications.

Therapists who intend to work with disabled people must develop an acute awareness of conscious and unconscious hindrances to their clients' dignity, and be mindful of any unconscious tendency to abuse the power inherent in the therapist's professional status. Offering a cure or the solution to problems is unhelpful in most psychotherapeutic relationships, and therapists who resort to such tactics become unavailable for their clients. Disabled clients' predicaments may touch upon the therapists' own vulnerability and death anxiety. Only when therapists are prepared to bear these uncomfortable feelings and appreciate their clients' experiences, will they become listeners and allies, rather than false saviours.'

2

A RELATIONAL MODEL OF DISABILITY

This chapter introduces the 'object relations construct of disability', or the 'relational model' for short. A model or construct is a representation of the whole or a part of a solid or abstract structure. The three main models of disability identified in disability studies are the medical model, the social model and the analytical model. The experience of disability and the variety of attitudes towards it are complex, and each of the disability models covers only part of this complexity: the medical model focuses on the body and its functions; the social model focuses on the interactions between disabled people as a minority group and the environment inhabited by the non-disabled majority; and the analytical model is concerned with the internal experience of disability. The relational model, which follows on from the analytical model, adds the missing element: the struggle through the developmental process towards interaction with the external world. We shall begin by considering the oldest and, I believe, most influential model.

The Medical Model

The medical model is based on a mind–body split, in which the body is regarded as a physiological system. It suggests that illness and disability are all about biochemical and physical malfunctions, or faults in need of correction. The medical profession is perceived both by its own members and by the public as a body whose role it is to cure what is defined as pathological or not normal. John Holland (1995), a general practitioner, writes about the unbearable impotence doctors feel in the presence of their patients' pain. He suggests that in defence doctors may attempt to deny reality and climb onto a pedestal labelled 'Excellent Carer'. By busying themselves with excessive care, their

19

patients are left feeling incompetent and powerless, while the doctors welcome the projection that they are all-powerful.

Beth, like many disabled people, is all too familiar with this dynamic. She was in her fifties when she was diagnosed as having multiple sclerosis (MS). When her consultant neurologist asked whether she had experienced any changes in her bodily functions she thought for a moment and than said, 'Yes, I don't empty my bowels as regularly as I used to'. The consultant decided to correct this 'abnormality' by means of a colostomy operation, which resulted in Beth's natural evacuation system being replaced by a colostomy bag. Beth was a quiet and passive person, and when she reported the change in her bodily routine she had only been trying to provide an answer to the consultant's question – it had not been her main concern. She had still been shaken by the MS diagnosis and struggling to find ways of coping. She had believed that her consultant would do only what was best for her. She had never thought of questioning his decision.

Several years later, during therapy, she said 'Why couldn't he let me be? I did not mind this irregular bowel movement it did not bother me. Now my life is a misery, sitting is becoming more and more uncomfortable, and this is a real problem because I am sitting in my wheelchair all day. But the worst thing is having to deal with the colostomy bag. Why did he do it to me?'

Beth's irregular functioning had not disturbed her, but it had disturbed her consultant. He had needed to ease his intolerable helplessness in the face of the incurable MS. He had needed to gain control, if not over the MS then at least over Beth's bowel movements. Restoring what seemed like control had been his way of dealing with the anxiety provoked by the unpredictable and the unknown. However his action also carries the message that disabled people are not accepted for what they are. They have to be 'normalised'.

While it should be remembered that medical advances are often very welcome and greatly appreciated by many disabled people, sometimes the hope invested in medical and scientific procedures ends up in disappointment and anger, which is then directed at the medical profession. The need to protect themselves against misdirected anger may offer some explanation of the secretive and distant manner of many in the medical profession. In Beth's case, her initial anger with her doctor provided an opening for her eventually to address her anger with MS, where upon she became she able to mourn and cope with her losses.

In her seminal book Deborah Marks (1999) suggests that the reason why health professionals sometimes fail to offer appropriate pain relief is that they cannot believe in and are therefore unable to empathise with their patients' experience of unbearable pain. This lack of belief, Marks explains, is often due to the lack of external evidence of pain, such as a visible injury. Why is a patient's pain not credible without external evidence? Perhaps it is because a visible injury can be treated and cured, thus relieving the doctor's anxiety about the suffering it has caused. When the cause of pain is unknown or untreatable, disbelief is a defence against helplessness.

LEARNING POINT

■ The medical model embraces the concept that disabled individuals should be 'repaired' so that they can function and look like the non-disabled majority.

The Social Model

In reaction against the medical model the disability movement developed a model based on the idea that the social environment should be changed to enable disabled people to function as equal members of society. The environment is seen as disabling because it discriminates against certain individual. Disabled people are seen as united by their shared experience of exclusion and prejudice. Rather than focusing on the impairments that distinguish disabled people from one another, the social model adopts a cross-disability perspective. Its main concern is to remove disabling environmental barriers and to increase disabled people's autonomy and choice.

Hanna, a wheelchair user, was invited to a meeting on the second floor of a building. She was told that there was a lift and thus assumed that the organisers of the meeting had ensured that access would not be difficult. However it proved impossible for her to operate the lift because the buttons were too high for her to reach. The underlying message Hanna received was 'This place is not designed for you. Although we have a lift, it is there for those who can reach the buttons, not for the likes of you, and you don't belong here.' Such experiences are an everyday occurrence for most disabled people.

The social model aims to change attitudes amongst the non-disabled majority so that inclusion will become the norm and impairment will not always be equated with disability (Oliver, 1990, 1996). Yet at times it may not be possible to create an environment that can address the needs of all disabled people because some people's needs conflict with others, for example some visually impaired people see better in bright light and others in dim light. In addition, if the social model is to be applied successfully we have to recognise, understand and address the collective fear that disability triggers (Menzies-Lyth, 1988).

Another factor that tends to be overlooked by advocates of the social model is what are called the 'secondary gains of disability': the tendency of some disabled people to develop a high degree of dependency and accept diminished autonomy. The words of Helen, who had to leave her work with the police due to arthritis, offer an explanation of this: 'This morning when I passed the bus stop and saw all these people waiting for the bus in the wind and rain I was glad I don't have to do it any more, I like it that the ambulance comes to pick me up from home.' Helen was speaking about the comfort she derived from her forced dependency – her loss of physical ability had been followed by loss of the will to 'fight it' out there. Her words highlight the thin and often unclear line that separates real needs from the seduction of dependency. As long as the focus of disability continues to be shifted away from the disabled individual onto society's attitudes, values and actions it is inevitable that the traits in Helen's somewhat regressive comment will tend to be ignored, because they may weaken the cause.

How can exclusion, whether intentional or through thoughtlessness, be turned into inclusion? The first step is to gain an understanding of the reasons behind exclusion, such as the survival instinct and death anxiety, as described in Chapter 1.

LEARNING POINT

■ Both the medical and the social model aim to 'cure' disability, the former by curing the impairment and the latter by curing the environment and social attitudes. This indicates that, despite the polarity of their views of the world and the opposing positions they occupy, both models aim to improve the state of disability.

The Analytical Model

The brief overview of the medical and social models of disability showed the different ways in which disability is conceptualised by disabled and non-disabled people. Both models are concerned with the external physical and social aspects of disability. Psychiatry, like any other medical profession, tends to deal with our innate helplessness in the face of suffering by focusing on symptom reduction. Psychoanalysis, on the other hand, sees symptoms as meaningful and removal of the symptoms is seen as closing the door on the opportunity to explore their causes. The analytical model is concerned with the internal experience of the disabled individual. Psychoanalysis views mental health as a continuum of experience in which there is both regression and progression. This inclusive approach has made an important contribution to our understanding of reactions to and defences against what is perceived as unbearable. Antipsychiatrists (such as Laing, Masson and others) and systems theorists (who are also influenced by psychoanalysis) maintain that mental health is not just an outcome of the individual's developmental history, but largely relates to the specific context in which the person lives and therefore cannot be understood in isolation. Emotional distress, dependency and other pathologies can be understood in terms of context, relationships and meanings. This is clearly relevant to understanding the effects of and reactions to disability.

Although limited attention is given to disability issues within psychoanalysis, one aspect that has been explored is the possible effect of body differences and impairment on the individual's psyche. Defence mechanisms such as denial and repression are seen as potentially useful in preventing the ego from being overwhelmed by anxiety. Since the body is the ego's first object, our body-self or body image is laden with archaic and prerepresentational meanings. Damage to the body, which is a source of self-identity and self-regard, can cause severe emotional upheaval, loss of identity and a diminished sense of self-worth.

Therapists and other professionals working with disabled people are consciously or unconsciously affected by the fear of disability and difference, which manifests itself in the countertransference. Countertransference is the term used to describe the emotional responses that the client triggers in the therapist. That is, any unresolved personal issues, conflicting values, biases and distortion can significantly affect the therapist's capacity to provide competent psychotherapy, or any other professional help.

Graeme Taylor (1994) has contributed to psychosomatic theory and the psychoanalytic approach to illness and disease with his 'dysregulation model'. This model is based on the concept that human beings are self-regulating cybernetic systems, each person comprising a hierarchy of subsystems that interact via the brain with the larger social system. According to this model, psychoanalytic intervention may favourably influence health not only by enhancing the regulatory capacity of the person's psyche, but also by modifying the reciprocal feedback it has with other subsystems. Clinical evidence that analytical treatment can positively affect the brain is reported by Viinamaki et al. (1998).

LEARNING POINTS

- Within the framework of disability, psychoanalysis explores the possible effects that physical differences and changes can have on the individual's psyche.
- The experience of the disabled individual can be understood in the specific context of the person's life, relationships and meanings.
- According to the dysregulation model the therapeutic relationship offers a regulatory system that can enhance both physical and mental health.

The Relational Model: the Object Relations Construct of Disability

The relational model points out the link between the experiences, both internal and external, of individuals who perceives themselves as disabled and the effects that disability can have on the non-disabled. Particular attention is given to the struggle against dependency and the stages by which disabled people achieve autonomy, a separate identity and a positive self-image. The concerns and difficulties experienced by disabled individuals are, of course, as varied and diverse as those of non-disabled people. However there are some factors that can be seen as disability specific. One such is the time of life at which disablement occurs, which can significantly influence the individual's adjustment process, self-perception and the way he or she is perceived by others. Therefore the model initially differentiates between congenital (present from birth) and acquired disability. There are four main constituents of the relational model:

- The developmental process from an object relations perspective.
- The perception of self.
- Identity, autonomy and separation.
- The perception of disability as an eternal transition and the construct of adolescence.

The developmental process from an object relations perspective

Freud's (1911) sequence of psychosexual stages was based on intrinsic developmental currents propelled by biological forces and on the predetermined maturation of needs. He did not consider that some of the stages he observed might have been cultural artefacts. Any developmental theory that is based, as are Freud's psychosexual stages, on the link between control over bodily functions and emotional maturity fails to address the way in which emotional maturity is achieved when body functioning is impaired. For example lack of bowel control or an inability to feed oneself will, according to the classical developmental stages, prevent the individual from reaching maturity.

While there has been little research on the effect of impairment on the developmental process, it is a fact that the great majority of disabled people achieve emotional maturity despite physical dependency. The growing power of the disability movement and the personal achievements of disabled individuals present a challenge to any theory that links physical functioning with emotional maturity. The writing and achievements of disabled people such as Brown (1954), McDonald (Crossley and McDonald, 1984), Nolan (1988), Davis (1989), Morris (1991), Greeley (1996), Shakespeare (Shakespeare et al., 1996), Olkin (1999) Keith (2001) and many others offer first-hand evidence that emotional maturity need not be dependent on physical independence. In this context emotional maturity has two main components:

- The person's awareness of his or her condition within the context of everyday life.
- The person's degree of separation from others, which manifests itself in the assumption of responsibility for his on her own well-being.

The relevance of object relations theory to disability

In the following paragraphs some aspects of the work of Klein (1932, 1948, 1975), Fairbairn (1952, 1954), Winnicott (1966, 1971, 1975c, 1986) and Mahler (1965; Mahler et al., 1975) will be reviewed in order to identify a perspective that could be used to understand the personality development and reactions of disabled people.

Melanie Klein

Klein, like Freud, believed that humans are motivated by drives. But unlike Freud she emphasised the early mother–child relationship and believed that aggression rather than sex was the primary instinct. She attached great importance to the child's relationship with the mother's breast, which as the primary object is alternately viewed as either ideal or persecutory. By implication, difficulty with feeding, sensing or touching, such as might be experienced by a disabled child, may influence the child's perceptions of the mother. According to Klein the child's sense of self as good or bad is related to the predominance of good and bad objects in its internal object world. Thus a breast that is perceived as predominantly bad due to difficulty adapting to the child's impairment will affect the latter's self-esteem.

In Kleinian theory projective identification is considered to be the main defence mechanism. This is the most primitive form of unconscious interaction, appearing at the earliest developmental stage when the child projects split-off parts of the self onto the caregiver and thus experiences and relates to the caregiver as if the latter were those parts. When a disabled child has difficulty with breast- or bottle-feeding, the caregiver's frustration about her lack of success nursing the child may be transmitted to the child, thus intensifying its feeling of persecution. Klein's observations on the early interactions between the child and the primary caregiver is supported by more recent evidence that the existence of a disability may affect these interactions (Brazelton *et al.*, 1974; Harkness and Super, 1994; Lussier, 1980; Threvanthen, 1985). Thus for those who choose a developmental perspective, Kleinian theory can be helpful in understanding the emotional problems associated with congenital disability.

W. R. D. Fairbairn

According to Fairbairn (1952, 1954) the child is born with a fully functioning, structured and unitary ego that deals with non-satisfying personal relationships with the use of defence mechanisms such as introjections of the non-satisfying object. Fairbairn conceptualised the non-satisfying object as having two sides: one that frustrates and one that tempts (see Buckley, 1986). Because the infant is unable to tolerate the situation, the non-satisfying object is split into two parts: an exciting object and a frustrating object. Both of these objects are repressed, eventually causing a splitting of the unitary ego. Following Fairbairn's theory we would not expect there to be differences in personality structure between people with disabilities and people without them, unless their disabilities prevented them from deriving satisfaction from their caregivers during childhood. In other words, only if a carergiver reacts differently to a child because the latter is disabled, for example by overcompensating or by coldness and avoidance can interpsychic conflict be expected to occur. Defence mechanisms such as splits in the object and splits in the ego are necessary only because of negative experiences imposed on the individual by an external object.

D. W. Winnicott

In Winnicott's (1975) view a child begins life in a state of psychologically undisturbed isolation. In this state the child makes spontaneous movements and the environment, which initially is the mother, is discovered without any loss of the sense of self. If the mother or primary caregiver fails to adapt to the child's needs the latter's sense of self is 'put into hiding'. Winnicott called the hidden self the true self, and argued that individuals develop a false self in order to face the world and protect the true self. The concept of true and false self is a critical aspect of Winnicott's (1965a) theory. The child develops a true self when there has been adequate adaptation to its needs. Conversely a false self develops when the child has to comply with the demands of caregivers and an environment that impinges upon it. When the child is disabled a false self may develop under the following circumstances:

- When the nature of the impairment makes it difficult for the caregiver to adapt adequately.
- When the caregiver's reaction to the child (for example repulsion, embarrassment or a feeling of hopelessness) is influenced by the disability.

At times the disability itself or the medical treatment involved can represent a significant environmental impingement, which may result in the child withdrawing psychologically, becoming isolated and hiding its true self.

Winnicott (1975a) introduced the concept of 'hate in the counter-transference', which refers to the natural tendency of mothers and therapists sometimes to hate their children and clients respectively, and to the importance of being able to accept, rather than repress, objective feelings of hate. The belief underlying this concept is that without objective hate there can be no objective love. From a developmental standpoint, in the case of a child with a disability a problem may arise if the caregiver overcompensates for natural feelings of objective hate, as this can leave the child without the capacity to love. The guilt associated with the hate felt towards the vulnerable child and reluctance to express the feeling can lead to inappropriate responses.

Margaret Mahler

Mahler believed that 'personhood' is not an innate given but has to be achieved through adaptation to the environment, which is personified by the mother. Mahler describes human development as an inter-psychic process whereby the child will eventually function on its own and not be helplessly dependent on the mother, but at the same time will retain an interpersonal tie to the mother. The separation/individuation process (Mahler *et al.*, 1975) is particularly complicated for infants with a disability due to their physical need for extra help and support. When the physical need for help remains almost unchanged, it may be difficult for both mother and infant to forge a distinct sense of identity. Some mothers of disabled children feel guilty about not preventing their child's predicament, and therefore tend to discourage attempts at separation and independence. Real concern and fear that the child may be injured can further complicate this problem.

LEARNING POINTS

■ Although the existing developmental models do not pay particular attention to the question of disability, some can be used as an adaptive framework. A particularly useful angle is offered by object relations theory, which views child development as an outcome of the relational environment.
■ The emphasis on interaction between individuals and their environment offers positive scope for understanding disabled people's developmental process.

Perception of self

Congenital disability

Based on the ideas developed by object relations and attachment theorists, the relational model maintains that an impaired body is not necessarily experienced by the disabled person as damaged or deformed (Lussier, 1960, 1980). Freud viewed the body ego as the main building block of the ego, which derives from self-perception. By what process, then, will individuals disabled from birth develop a perception of their body? Much of the available literature and the clinical material presented in this book suggest that most people with a congenital disability perceive their body as a whole, integrated object rather than as incomplete.

For example, during his analysis of Peter, who had very short and deformed arms, Lussier (1960) noted that the boy was adamant about using his arms as they were, rather than wearing artificial limbs. With great perseverance young Peter succeeded in mastering bicycle riding and playing the trumpet. His determination was fuelled by the belief that his body was a good, whole body. He wanted to be accepted by others as he really was rather then as a person with an incomplete body. Likewise Di, who will be discussed in Chapter 5, preferred to struggle with her very limited and unclear speech than replace it with the computerised speech emitted from the computer she had accepted as a temporary aid for the benefit of others. She perceived herself as a whole person with impaired speech, rather then an incomplete person dependent on a computer.

While the disabled infant initially perceives its body as whole, the primary caregiver, usually the mother, may find it difficult to do likewise. She may need to overcome strong feelings of disappointment, loss and grief, which in turn may evoke guilt, shame or anger. When the primary caregiver is able to deal with her initial reactions and accept the child for what he or she is, then the child will receive the holding and containment necessary for the development of a positive sense of self. Kohut (1984, p. 21) argues that the fear and anxiety evoked by 'the mother whose face does not light up at the sight of her child' is a most dreadful and damaging experience.

LEARNING POINTS

■ The infant's initial perception of its body is of a whole, good object regardless of impairment.
■ The attachment bond and level of 'attunement' that develop between mother and infant during the early stage of infancy form the basis of all subsequent object relationships and self-perception.

Acquired disability

When a non-disabled person becomes disabled it can feel like being thrown into an unknown, alien territory for which there is no map. In order to adjust to the change it is necessary to develop a new view of the self and a new view of the world. The first step is to recognise that the functioning of the body and perhaps its shape have been altered. The impact of the unexpected change in body shape and function often activates a defence against the unbearable implications of the injury or disease. Denying the change or aspects of it is a defence against fragmentation of the self.

Anosognosia, which was first observed and named by the French neurologist Babinski is the tendency to ignore or deny paralysis. An extreme case of this is described by Oliver Sacks (1984). A man kept falling out of bed at night. Each time he crashed to the floor the ward staff would lift him back into bed, only to hear a resounding thud a few minutes later. Sacks asked the man why he kept falling out of bed. 'Doctor', the man said, 'these medical students have been putting a cadaver's leg in my bed and I have been trying to get rid of it all night.' The man was refusing to admit ownership of his paralysed leg, and was being propelled onto the floor each time he tried to throw it away. Such denial serves to preserve the individual's sense of continuity, stability and cohesion by encapsulating the traumatic experience away from the conscious mind.

A comparison of dreams reported in therapy indicates that people with a congenital disability rarely dream about their disability, while people who have acquired a disability later in life often refer to their dream life as a predisability space. 'This morning I woke up again into a nightmare', Beth would often tell me. 'In my dream I was dancing, and look at me now, I can't even walk.' Stan, who had lost his sight in his late forties, was bitterly disappointed when he woke into a world veiled by blindness after dreaming he was his old sighted self. The newly disabled person has to struggle with the task of accepting and integrating a new body image. When Beth described her waking life as a nightmare, she was implying that part of her psyche had not adapted to the change and perhaps never would, that there was still an expectation of awakening into a predisability reality.

Ali, an Afro-Caribbean man in his sixties, had been suffering from multiple sclerosis for ten years. When I saw him he was unable to walk and was using a wheelchair. He felt that he was a victim of a terrible mistake: 'How come I have MS when it is well known that Afro-Caribbean people don't get MS?' Ali's emotional life oscillated between denial and rage. His reaction to MS was to throw all his medication down the toilet, hoping that the disease would be flushed away with the pills. When his wife visited family or friends he refused to join her, saying that he did not want to be in the company of people who would laugh at him because of his wheelchair. Ali imprisoned himself at home, apart from his twice-weekly visits to the MS Club. In the club's therapy group Ali would punch his thighs, saying 'Why can't you stupid legs let me walk, you useless things.'

Newly disabled people such as Beth, Ali and Stan have to struggle to piece together the fragments of their past and their present in order to retain some stability and maintain continuity with their sense of self. This process is similar to that undergone by refugees who have been forced to flee their beloved homeland.

LEARNING POINTS

■ The onset of disability forces newly disabled people out of the non-disabled world to face the task of bridging the gap between their present reality and their pre-expulsion, predisability experiences.

■ A unique combination of factors affects the self-perception of all newly disabled individuals, including their belief system, predisability experiences, self-esteem and the nature of their medical condition. There are also external factors, such as the reaction of their social group and how accommodating their physical environment is.

Comparing congenital and acquired disability

When I asked Dina, a trainee counsellor who had been blind since birth, to work with people who had become blind or were losing their sight, she said 'But I am not blind'. 'What do you mean?' I asked. Dina explained that because she had never experienced being sighted she had never become blind. Her perception of herself as 'not seeing' was an integral part of her self-image and identity. She was aware that there was a profound difference between her experience of blindness and that of people who had lost their sight later in life. Dina was living in the world of the sighted and was acutely aware of her lack of sight, of which she was reminded numerous times a day when she bumped into a chair that had been left in the middle of the room or missed the bus because she had not seen it coming. She may have had an idea of what it was like to see, but it remained a fantasy, outside her own identity and self-image.

In contrast Stan, who had lost his sight as an adult, was struggling to integrate past and present. His experience, knowledge and memories still largely belonged to the seeing part of his life. Although he was no longer able to see, his self-image as a sighted person still accounted for a major part of his identity.

One difference between the two groups has to do with the 'what if' or the 'filling in' phenomenon; that is, the way in which nature, including the human mind, reacts to a vacuum by supplying whatever information is required to complete the scene (Ramachandran, 1998). People with a congenital disability practice 'conceptual filling in'. For example one day I said to Dina, 'That's a nice shirt you are wearing', to which she replied, 'Oh, yes, thank you, I do like blue'. This threw me a bit, so I said 'Dina, what is "Blue" for you?' 'Oh', she said, 'it is a cool, peaceful, relaxing colour', and she went on to explain how she had developed, through her other senses and from reading, her own subjective concepts of colour, proportion and other visual notions.

People with an acquired disability tend to practice 'perceptual filling in'. Clare, who was 38, had lost her sight at 15. In therapy she talked about her compulsive need to rearrange the furniture in her house. Her visualisation and knowledge of what the furniture arrangements looked like were based on her early experiences of visual perception. Clare could not check the representations of an object against the object itself because she was blind, so the lack of sensory feedback created a vacuum in which her visual memory had no boundaries or limitations. Her obsessive compulsion was an attempt to gain some control by continually manipulating actual objects. This has some similarity to the phantom limb phenomenon, in which the brain holds on to sensations of pain from a missing limb but the pain cannot easily be controlled because there is no feedback from the missing limb.

LEARNING POINTS

■ Both newly disabled people and those with a congenital impairment may experience envy, rage and a sense of loss. These stem from their perception of themselves as different, due to their impaired body or their disabling social and physical environment.
■ The world in which the members of both groups live is not yet ready to accept and embrace their difference hence everyday functioning is studded with attitudinal and physical obstacles that exacerbate their sense of alienation.

To be or not to be disabled?

Identity, autonomy and separation

Disabled children are born into exile, unsure of whether or not they belong with the people inhabiting their home environment. Yet unlike people in exile, who can hold on to their memories of their homeland, people who have been born with an impairment have no 'lost homeland' to dream about. In his much-loved tale *The Ugly Duckling* (1928) the Danish author Hans Christian Andersen describes the suffering endured by a duckling who was not a duckling at all but a cygnet, and was rejected for being different. The mother duck's attempts to protect him were unsuccessful; she could not stop the aggressive hostility provoked by his unusual appearance so he was forced to flee in search of his own kind.

Like the duckling; most disabled children experience life from a different perspective from that of their parents and siblings. But unlike the duckling it is not always clear who their own kind is. There is rarely an available role model to look up to and identify with, so disabled children are constantly reminded that they are different. Regardless of how much their family and relations accept and love them being a stranger without peers or a reference group can hinder the development of their identity and sense of self.

In the preface to her book *What Psychotherapist Should Know About Disability* Rhoda Olkin (1999, p. vii) writes: 'I am bicultural. I live in two worlds – the nondisabled majority and my minority group's world of the disability community.' Olkin tells us that for 30 years she desperately tried to pass herself off as normal despite the effects of childhood polio, but eventually she managed to admit to herself (others knew it already) that she was a person with a disability. Discovering her own peer group in the disability movement brought great relief.

The desire to pass oneself off as normal has been stimulated in recent years by scientific advances in pregnancy screening. The purpose of screening is to gain information about the unborn baby and to identify conditions such as spina bifida, Down's syndrome and others. Such information may then be used to decide whether to continue or terminate the pregnancy. People affected by one of these conditions may be deeply disturbed by the idea that if their mother had been screened and found out about their condition the pregnancy might well have been terminated. It therefore follows that being diagnosed as having a medical condition and then being identified as disabled may well feel unsafe, as illustrated by the way in which Joe, the eight-year-old discussed in Chapter 4, became alarmed and angry when I implied that he was disabled. This threat and the anxiety it evokes may also be linked to the archaic wish to eliminate disability, as discussed in Chapter 1. This may inhibit the development of a unified self-perception that acknowledges and includes the impairment. It is hardly surprising that some disabled people do not want to be identified as such, given their awareness that discovery of their impairment *in utero* could have brought about the termination of their existence.

'The community of persons with disability has an open enrolment – anyone can join at anytime by acquiring a disability' (Olkin, 1999, p. 32). The irony here stems from the assumption that most people do not want to join the disabled community but it is a one-way ticket, that is, disabled people are not welcome to join the community of non-disabled.

LEARNING POINTS

- Although most disabilities are visible, accepting oneself as disabled is often the final stage of a long process of gaining self-knowledge and making relational adjustments.
- Society's fear of disabilities and the measures taken to eliminate them is yet another obstacle to disabled people accepting disability as part of their identity.

Continuity of the sense of self

The experience of becoming disabled during adolescence or adulthood can sever or damage the individual's sense of historical continuity with the past, perhaps splitting off the perception of the self into two: the good non-disabled past, and the bad disabled present. Melanie Klein (1952) describes this as an aspect of the paranoid-schizoid position, which may cause regression into an earlier developmental stage. The concept of adolescence, used in understanding the maturation process of non-disabled people, may offer a way of understanding this aspect of the disabled person's experience and a way of thinking about the possibility of bridging this past–present split of the self.

For people who have been disabled since birth or early infancy there may not have been an event to trigger regression or arrested development. Yet such people are often perceived by themselves and others as being stuck in adolescence, either never experiencing full adulthood or only having occasional short sorties into adulthood before regressing back. It therefore seems that an understanding of adolescence could give us insights into the adaptive process disabled people have to go through.

Disability as eternal transition

The theoretical framework of the relational model utilises the concept of adolescence to conceptualise the process of transition and change. Adolescence is the name given to the transitional period in which the dependent child is expected to prepare to become an independent adult. It is a period in which freedom, autonomy and responsibility are exercised and tested in preparation for mature adulthood.

The ways in which individuals conceptualise their bodies have preoccupied theorists and researchers in areas other then psychology. The French philosopher Merleau-Ponty (1962) suggests that the concept of the perfect body held in the mind is the 'wished for body' or the body as a whole, as opposed to the 'body in the moment', which is the body we actually possess, with all its imperfections. In the field of medical research, the Canadian neurosurgeons Penfield (Penfield and Rasmussen, 1950) and Perot (1963) suggest that there is a representation of the body on the surface of the brain, that is, the brain holds a 'map' of the body. Current brain scanning techniques, which have greatly improved since the days of Penfield's pioneering work, offer evidence of the existence of such a body map. The working hypothesis is that both the brain and the unconscious mind expect our own bodies and other bodies to which we relate to have the full complement of components. Thus the sight of incompleteness causes disturbance. The incompleteness of the immature baby's body is accepted because in time it will become complete. Conceptualising impairment or disability as a temporary phase stems from the hope that the next developmental stage will clear away the impairment, that time will heal. Therefore disabled people tend to be perceived by others and sometimes by themselves as having been arrested at the transitional, adolescent stage.

LEARNING POINT

■ Disability tends to be perceived, consciously or unconsciously, as a transitional phase. Therefore the concept of the adolescent phase is proposed as a thinking framework.

Parenting a disabled child

Throughout childhood the parents of disabled children and the children themselves may hold on to the hope that the impairment will disappear as they grow up, like milk teeth and childhood illnesses. Looking after disabled children during infancy is in many respects similar to looking after non-disabled children as all are entirely dependent on their caregiver. However during early adolescence, when the children are supposed to be preparing to become young adults, both the parents and the young people are faced with the realisation that the disability is not likely to go away, it is there to stay. The hope, no matter how dim or unconscious, of it disappearing slowly fades, leaving all parties feeling dejected. This is one of the main times when the parents of disabled children are likely to need emotional support. They have coped well enough with the specific needs and demands of their children, but now they find themselves at a confusing crossroads, unsure which direction to take. Are they expected to care for the children forever, or should they let them find their own way? They often need a place to think about their love for and care of their children, as well as the resentment and anger about the effect that the children have had on their lives. Some parents defend themselves against uncertainty, guilt and anxiety by treating the disabled young people as though they will remain forever in a child-like state. In later chapters I shall describe the experiences of people such as Lynn, who at the age of 29 was not allowed to dye her hair, Maria, who was left sexually ignorant, and Ron, who was afraid of his dead mother. These and other stories offer us an insight into the emotional complexity of the arena in which many young disabled people struggle for autonomy.

LEARNING POINT

■ Parenting a disabled child requires a complicated and delicate balance between encouraging autonomy and independence while providing the necessary care and support.

The challenge of adolescent tasks

Adolescence is an in-between state that is often seen as the second individuation process (Blos, 1967). It is a transitional time in which young people prepare to embrace the autonomy and responsibility of adulthood and to let go of the security, familiarity and dependency of childhood. For non-disabled young people autonomy is a natural outcome of completion of the difficult tasks of adolescence. For some disabled people, however, the challenge of completing these tasks may at times seem insurmountable.

Task one

The first task is to disengage from parental figures, both as love objects and as authority figures, and to accept ownership of one's body and responsibility for one's actions. This task has two stages.

Stage one: disengagement from the parental figure. In addition to the separation difficulties experienced by many non-disabled youngsters, disabled youngsters are faced with confusion and ambivalence about the practical process of disengaging. Non-disabled youngsters are expected to spend unsupervised time learning how to negotiate their own place in the world by measuring their strength against that of peers, as well as communicating, developing relationships and exploring their sexuality. Most disabled people are rarely left unsupervised, either by their parents, their carers or other professionals. Without some degree of privacy it is difficult to develop peer relationships and put social skills to the test. Deprived of 'behind the bike shed' experiences, whether real or metaphorical, disabled people do not have the opportunity to experiment, explore their sexuality or exchange information. Due to their limited peer-group contact they are usually more dependent on and have a more involved and intense relationship with their parents and carers than do non-disabled people.

In the therapeutic setting, in order to understand the way in which their clients' self-image and body image have evolved, therapists have to identify and familiarise themselves with the factors that are con-tributing to their clients' difficulty with disengaging from parental authority figures, especially restrictions on interpersonal relationships. The parents of disabled adolescents may be torn between a desire to protect the latter and compensate for the impairment, and a desire for them to find a place in the world. The success of the disengagement processes depends to a large degree on the extent to which parents are able to resolve this conflict. Even adult clients can be affected by unre-solved parental guilt, shame or anger. Outside the therapeutic arena, support facilities and practical help play an important part in enabling or obstructing the task of disengagement.

Stage two: Accepting ownership of one's body and responsibility for one's reactions. For the adolescent this stage is the culmination of the period of growth, during which their bodies have been subject to constant physiological change. At times they may have felt out of control, which may have challenged their sense of ownership of and responsibility for their bodies. However, once the changes slow down and the body reaches equilibrium they are ready for this ownership and responsibility. Yet for disabled people the task of owning the body and assuming responsibility can prove particularly difficult and confusing. For example when involuntary movement or incontinence are part of a condition, what does responsibility mean? The task for each individual is to develop a definition of responsibility and ownership that reflects the reality of their medical condition, their social and cultural setting and their mental and emotional state. We should not forget that it was not so long ago that dependence on a servant for bathing and dressing was normal part of life for the aristocracy. The difference, of course, is that they had the physical ability to look after themselves but chose to allow another to do it, while a paralysed person has no such choice. The therapeutic task is therefore to identify and explore the ways in which clients can assume ownership of and responsibility for their bodies within the given reality.

Task two

The second task is to let go of the wish to change the unchangeable. It is questionable whether this task can or should ever be fully completed. Who decides what is and what is not changeable? Is the wish to undergo orthopaedic or cosmetic surgery in order to improve the functioning or appearance of the body an indication of an incomplete task of adolescence? Is the wish to change the attitudes of others part of this task? Rather than letting go of the wish to change it might be better to develop the capacity to engage in an ongoing evaluation of wishes and aspirations. Christopher Reeves, the actor who played Superman and was paralysed in a riding accident, is putting a great deal of energy into his fight to change the unchangeable by looking for a treatment that will enable him to walk again. Is this result of being stuck in the second task of adolescence, or is he holding on to hope because otherwise the situation would be unbearable for him? At the other end of the spectrum is Ali, who refused to believe that he had contracted MS and disassociated himself from it by hiding his paralysed legs.

The therapist's task in such situations is to evaluate with each individual the consequences of holding on to or letting go of their seemingly unrealistic wish. This task also reflects an aspect of the mourning process, which is intrinsic to acknowledgement of being in the world, to withdrawing emotional energy from what is expected and investing it in what is there.

Task three

The third tasks is to ensure continuity with the past. There is a somewhat paradoxical element to this task, which is about holding on to something that is no more. A ritualistic structure such as mourning can offer a useful framework for maintaining continuity with the past. A difficult but essential part of the maturation process is developing a willingness to acknowledge pain and sadness while letting go of unfulfilled hopes and desires. Developing the ability to recognise the past as part of oneself while at the same time living in the present and looking forward to the future can prove a challenge to some disabled people and those affected by their disability, such as their parents. It is a balance between becoming stuck in the past, like Ali, and severing links with it altogether. Ali turned away from the flow of his life in the present because he could not let go of his desire to walk. Parents who reject their disabled child as a defence against the pain of not having their wished-for child are trying to sever links with the past.

Continuity with the past means keeping the links alive while moving forward. People who acquire a disability later in life can find this task particularly difficult as they have to find a way of connecting their past non-disabled self with the present disabled self. For many people the onset of disability, whether through illness or accident, is a trauma for which the defence system is ill-equipped. When the defence system is not able to digest an event the psyche attempts to encapsulate it away from the conscious memory. This process breaks the continuity of being.

The therapeutic task here is to gain an understanding of the way in which the traumatic event has affected the client in order to bridge the chasm between the difficult reality and the hopes of the past.

Task four

The fourth task is to consolidate gender identity and sexual preference. The process of sexual development is fundamentally the same whether the individual is disabled or not. The main stumbling block for disabled people is the the way in which they are perceived and related to by others, either as asexual beings or as oddities. However, even when they are accepted as ordinary sexual beings, disabled people are faced with a mass of practical obstacles to exploring their sexuality and forming sexual relationships.

Consider the following scenario. The fire alarm goes off in the middle of the night in two establishments: a residential school for disabled young people and a boarding school for the non-disabled. How many young people would emerge from a room that was not their own in each of the schools? It is safe to assume that no one in the school for the disabled would be where they should not be, but that quite a few in the school for the non-disabled would be in someone else's room. The reason for the lack of experimentation and risk taking amongst some disabled people could be the result of internalising the perceptions of and attitudes towards their sexuality presented by their parents, the media and other sources. (Chapter 6 further investigates the issue of disability and sexuality.)

The therapeutic task here is to raise awareness of the role of physical and emotional courage and of the possibility of challenging authority and exploring relationships and sexuality.

LEARNING POINTS

- Regardless of the client's chronological age he or she may still be struggling with unfinished tasks of adolescence, which can cause confusion about identity and self-image.
- The four tasks of adolescence, as described by Blos (1967), offer the therapist a useful developmental framework for facilitating the maturation process.
- People who were born with an impairment may never have had the necessary encouragement to grow up and reach adulthood, while people who have acquired a disability later in life may find themselves regressing into adolescence because they have not been prepared for life as a disabled adult.

Summary

This chapter has considered the ideas that directly or indirectly underpin clinical practice with people affected by disability. The medical model concentrates on the possibility of change, while the social model addresses equality and inclusion by viewing disability as a social construct. The preferred psychoanalytical approach is the object relations construct of disability, or relational model, as presented by Klein, Fairbairn Winnicott and Mahler. Its emphasis on early childhood interactions between children and their primary caregivers offers a paradigm for understanding the emotional development of disabled people. The relational model is based on the concept of transition. It takes the conflicts, difficulties and achievements that characterise the tasks of adolescence as a useful organisational structure for understanding disability. Autonomy, identity and separation are recognised as the main elements of the ongoing transitional process.

Therapists who work with people affected by disability may be encouraged by the idea that the personal and emotional effects of disability and environmental impingements can be worked through if the therapeutic relationship is well held and contained.

Disability and the Practice of Psychotherapy

This chapter explores the therapist's task of managing the therapeutic relationship. The opening vignette draws attention to issues relating to the initial contact and assessment, and examines aspects of this that have particular relevance for disabled people. Respect by the therapist for the client is a necessary precondition for the formation of a positive relationship and enhancement of the client's autonomy. The vignettes illustrate the complexity of working with a client whose physical dependency necessitates a high level of care and medical intervention. The role of the therapist as the client's ally will be compared and contrasted with that of other carers and health professionals.

The First Contact

The duty counsellor's phone rang. On the other end of the line a woman asked 'Do you do counselling for disabled people? I need to arrange therapy for my daughter.' Without waiting for a reply she spoke about the family's recent return from Switzerland to England and her daughter's rare and complicated medical condition (disonomia). The duty counsellor asked how old the daughter was in order to ascertain whether she was still under parental guardianship. Lynn was 29 years old so the counsellor explained that the first step in the referral procedure was for the prospective client to contact the service in person.

The next day Lynn phoned the agency to ask for an appointment, but when it came to arranging the time and venue she handed the phone over to her mother. when Lynn arrived for her first appointment she was in a wheelchair and her mother was pushing her. The therapist opened the door for Lynn to enter, where upon the mother expectantly asked the therapist, 'Do you want me to come in?' Rather then responding to the mother the therapist turned to Lynn and said 'Lynn, this is your therapy time, you can decide how you want to use it.' Before Lynn had time to reply her mother spoke about Lynn's medical condition and its manifestations, to which the therapist said, 'I believe Lynn will tell me as much as she wants me to know.' Lynn then said 'I will stay on my own.' She got out of the wheelchair and wheeled it into the consulting room. The wheelchair was never again brought to therapy.

Once in the room, Lynn said 'Sometimes I feel very upset, but I can't be upset at home, my parents don't like it. My mother is very worried about me; she would not allow me to dye my hair like my cousin does. She says it is too dangerous; it may hurt my eyes.' After a deep sigh she added, 'What's the point of it all, if I can't do anything I like?'

The above is a short example of the process that culminates in the first contact between client and therapist. But picking up the phone to ask for therapy is not the beginning of the process, so what is the starting point? What leads to the first contact? What motivates people to seek therapy? Individual clients will have a different answer to these questions, but in each case the process begins long before the first session.

The reason for contacting a therapist usually falls into one of two categories: the individual is experiencing internal or external difficulties that are more than she or he can cope with alone; or the individual is seeking personal growth and a better insight into her or his mental and emotional processes, often as a part of a training programme. Ultimately, however, the two are not mutually exclusive: people who enter therapy for a specific problem may also gain insight into their internal processes beyond that problem, while students who enter therapy only to fulfil a training requirement may uncover hidden problems.

LEARNING POINTS

■ The way in which the first contact is managed becomes an integral part of the therapeutic relationship.
■ A disabled person may experience more difficulty with and be more hesitatant about seeking therapy.

Assessment

Psychotherapists differ in respect of theory and practice. There currently exist hundreds of approaches to counselling and psychotherapy, all of which are aimed at finding a useful and workable way of alleviating suffering and bringing about a better quality of life. Some of these approaches focus on specific client groups. The rationale for dividing clients into groups varies a great deal, ranging from the need of professionals to categories to the wish of specific interest groups to assert their group identity. Disabled people may find themselves categorised both by professionals and by movements and organisations of disabled people. Throughout this book the term 'disabled people' is applied to people with some kind of impairment, but this might be all they have in common as in other respects they represent the full cross-section of society.

Assessment is widely used to categorise people, but what is the rationale for using it in psychotherapy? Moreover what do we mean by 'assessment'? According to *The Shorter Oxford English Dictionary* it is 'Evaluation, estimation, an estimate of worth'. The notion of assessment in psychotherapy covers a range of acknowledged and unacknowledged purposes and intentions. It is not always clear whose needs are being served by the assessment: is it aimed at finding out what is best for the client, or is it a defence mechanism by which therapists and organisations protect themselves from the suffering that clients bring to their doorstep?

In psychotherapy 'assessment' is akin to the medical diagnostic process. But unlike medical diagnosis it is not always clear what is being assessed. Is it the client's mental health, background or ability to participate in a therapeutic relationship? If all three, in which order or combination? How can, some or all of these aspects of the client, which are not clearly defined or agreed upon, be assessed in a single session?

Another issue that requires further investigation stems from the ongoing debate on the indicators and knowledge base that inform psychotherapeutic diagnosis: is it possible to integrate intuition, information and systematic method into a reliable and useful assessment process?

There are several schools of thought on the purpose of assessment and the way to conduct it, the latter ranging from an interrogative exercise where the assessor asks a fixed set of questions, to what amounts to a mini therapeutic session. Hinshelwood (1991) proposes a 'trial interpretation', where the assessor conducts the interview as a mini session. When the preceding contacts are viewed as part of the therapeutic process, the assessment will reflect that process and will indeed be like a mini session. A reliable way of finding out whether people are able and willing to make use of the therapist's skills and expertise is to give them a sample of it rather then bombarding them with questions. In this method the assessor starts with a question such as 'What brings you here?', 'Where would you like to start?' or 'How can I be of help?', but from then on he or she listens and interprets as in any other session.

Some therapists feel that transference interpretations, in which the therapist comments on the client's perception of the therapist and relates this to early relationships, should be avoided during the assessment session, especially if the assessor intends to refer the client to another therapist. This view is based on the assumption that transference is unique to the therapeutic encounter.

As indicated, transference is the transfer to the therapist from the client of emotions previously directed at another person or thing. When human beings engage with other people the presence of the latter triggers conscious or unconscious associations, which then affect the way in which they are perceived. Although we do not call it transference in everyday interactions, the choice of what to communicate contains a comment on the other, as well as the actual information.

Let us look at Lynn's comment after her mother had reluctantly left the therapy room: 'Sometime I feel very upset'. At that point it would have been helpful and appropriate for the therapist to offer an interpretation that acknowledged Lynn's perception of the therapist as upsetting the mother as well as sharing Lynn's feelings about her parents. Such an interpretation would have offered Lynn a taste of what the psychotherapeutic relationship was about, an experience that would enable her to tell whether this was what she was looking for. As for the therapist, Lynn's reaction to the interpretation would have indicated whether she was ready to receive this form of therapy.

As well as assessing the client's ability to engage in a therapeutic relationship, the assessment procedure could form part of a defence mechanism in which the assessor serves as a gatekeeper to protect the interests of the system rather then those of the client. Thinking of the assessment process as a diagnosis brings with it the sense of certainty that is attached to some aspects of medicine, where clearly defined diagnostic tools are used and the outcome is seen as predictable. This assumption of certainty and the power to cure help to reduce the anxiety triggered by the uncertainty of facing a new and unknown client.

A different concept of assessment is of a natural process that commences whenever two people meet for the first time, and is not limited to the one or more sessions allocated to the task. It is an ongoing, two-way process in which two strangers, in our case the client and the therapist/assessor, assess each other. In his or her mind the client formulates a view of the organisation and the therapist, but may have been anticipating what it will be like to engage in therapy long before the first session/assessment. The client's premeeting assessment is based on a combination of written information, phone calls and perhaps some discussion with the referring agent. The assessor may also have started the process by communicating with or about the client, for example by phone, a written referral or a letter.

LEARNING POINTS

- The purposes and practice of assessments are varied and changeable.
- To avoid misuse of assessments, the usefulness and appropriateness of the assessment method should be subject to regular evaluation.
- The process of assessment and evaluation continue throughout the therapeutic relationship.

Managing the First Session

The wish to help

When the therapist first saw Lynn she felt a desire to take care of Lynn and make her better, to take away this awful condition that had stunted her growth and left her so fragile and vulnerable. The therapist's inability to bring about a physical change caused frustration and a sense of helplessness. Becoming aware of and acknowledging this not only prevented mismanagement of the relationship, but also gave the therapist a glimpse into Lynn's on going experiences and created a common ground for understanding her predicament Therapists, like other care workers, experience an internal struggle between the omnipotent wish to make a difference by appearing strong and able and the awareness that acknowledging one's own limitations and frustrations is a prerequisite for empathy and understanding. When therapists are able to let go of the fantasy of being a saviour they arrive at a more realistic perception. They become aware that their task is not to change or improve their clients' physical condition, but to participate in a mutual process in which the clients will be helped to develop their autonomy. By letting go of the fantasy of control the therapists may find themselves confronted not only by their clients' helplessness and vulnerability but also by their own. The discomfort caused by close proximity to the fragility of human existence is probably the main reason why many therapists refrain from working with disabled people.

Third-party involvement

Because disabled people are sometimes perceived as incomplete there is a tendency to fill in the missing parts by bringing in elements external to the therapeutic dyad. These elements are referred to as 'third party'.

Let us look again at the initial contact with Lynn. The first call was made by the mother, who presumably took charge because she did not believe that her daughter was capable of doing so. She also informed the duty counsellor that Lynn's medical condition was the reason, why she needed counselling. At that point confusion could have arisen as to who was actually seeking help. It is not unusual for a referral to be made by a relative who is unconsciously seeking counselling for him- or herself but is not yet ready to admit it. Challenging Lynn's mother on her motive, would not have been productive and could have resulted in unnecessary tension and heightened defences. Instead the counsellor, who had been trained to deal with confused and worried relatives, simply explained the referral procedure, which in order to promote client autonomy usually requires the prospective client to contact the service directly.

Another approach would have been to offer family therapy, in which the family would be treated as a unit and its dynamics and interactions explored and explained. The reason for not offering family therapy when the original request is for individual therapy is that a disabled person often needs help with issues such as impaired autonomy and a blurred sense of self. For disabled people, natural separation from parental figures is often delayed due to the complexity of the practical and emotional issues involved. Their need to experience a private space of their own is often best addressed initially through individual therapy. Then, when appropriate, family therapy could be suggested as a follow-up.

When Lynn eventually did contact the service herself she was not ready to take charge and quickly handed over the phone and control to her mother. This was the first evidence of her inner conflict between autonomy and dependency. Therapists who become aware of such conflicts, either directly when taking the initial call or indirectly through the duty counsellor, organise their thinking around this conflict. When Lynn and her mother arrived at the counselling centre the mother, still in control, tried to push both Lynn and herself, physically and symbolically, into the first session. This was a difficult moment for the therapist, who was meeting mother and daughter for the first time and was unsure of the dynamics between them.

It is clear that mutual dependency played a major part in this mother–daughter–therapist triad. When the mother asked 'Do you want me to come in?' the therapist felt as if she was walking on a tightrope, with Lynn's autonomy as the client at one end and the mother's position as the principal carer at the other. However as Lynn was identified both by her mother and by herself as the client it was clear that initially a dyad rather than a triad needed to be established.

The options open to the therapist in respect of managing the first meeting were as follows:

- To let the mother in and approach the therapeutic work from a systemic, family perspective.
- To say to the mother something along the lines of 'I am sorry, but only Lynn can come into the room.'
- To put Lynn in charge of the decision.

We shall look at the advantages and disadvantages of each of these options in turn.

First, having both Lynn and her mother in the room would have given the therapist an opportunity to observe the dynamics of the mother–daughter relationship, which might have offered some understanding of Lynn's everyday life. By agreeing to the mother's request the therapist would have promoted a positive relationship with her, Lynn's main carer, and obtained information about Lynn that might have lessened the anxiety of working with an unknown client. As for the mother, she would have received a degree of counselling by proxy. Any therapist who chose to include the mother would have needed to think long and hard about how and why a request for individual therapy had turned into family work. Lynn's space, time and relationships were already controlled for her, and going along with the mother's desire to be present would have meant that Lynn's need to gain control and develop her autonomy would have been pushed to the side.

Second, the therapist's clear assertion that only Lynn could enter the room could have made Lynn feel that at long last she had an ally, a professional who was on her side rather then her mother's. It would also have made clear to the mother and Lynn that the therapeutic frame was strong and non-negotiable, and therefore reliable. On the other hand, if the therapist had made the decision for Lynn she might have perpetuated Lynn's dependency by exchanging a controlling mother for a controlling therapist.

Third, in the end the therapist decided to take a calculated risk and give the decision-making power to Lynn. The risk was related to the fact that this was the first meeting and Lynn would be the therapist's sole source of information. Furthermore, she did not know how Lynn would respond to the power and trust invested in her, and how it would affect her relationship with her mother.

When the therapist told Lynn that this was her therapy time and she could decide how to use it, the mother, obviously feeling somewhat excluded, reacted immediately by giving instructions relating to Lynn's medical condition – she used her knowledge of and involvement with Lynn's condition to assert her own importance. The therapist, in keeping with her decision to foster autonomy in Lynn, turned to the mother and said, 'I believe Lynn will tell me as much as she wants me to know.' This comment served to establish the basis of the therapeutic relationship:

- From then on only Lynn and the therapist would take part in the therapeutic relationship; there would be no third party to cause confusion.
- Lynn was an adult and that was how she would be related to in the therapy.
- The therapy would focus on Lynn and not on her medical condition. The therapist did not need to know all the details of it.

Hence the therapist's efforts were directed at establishing Lynn's status as an adult and offering Lynn a space in which to exercise her autonomy. Her response 'I will stay on my own' indicated that she was willing to try to let go of her dependency on her mother. Her getting out of the wheelchair can be interpreted as 'I need the support of the wheelchair at times, but I want to be the one who controls it.' Lynn's first comment in the session – 'Sometimes I feel very upset' – was possibly triggered by the difficulty of having to choose between mother and therapist, a little like a child having to let go of her mother on the first day of school.

Despite the pain of separation, Lynn desperately wanted to be like any other young woman, which she indicated by her expressed wish to be allowed to dye her hair, as her cousin had done. She had asked for help because her attempt to become an autonomous adult had been thwarted by parental anxiety and over-care. Although she knew that at times her condition could threaten her life, it is important to note that the first issue she raised was not to do with her disability or medical condition but with difficulties in her relationship with her parents, particularly her mother's anxiety.

LEARNING POINTS

- A clearly thought-out practice policy accompanied by well-structured procedures offer a supportive frame for both therapist and client.
- When a disabled person requests individual therapy it is important to respect this wish, and to overcome the temptation to introduce others into the therapeutic relationship.

External information as an aspect of the third party

Why did the therapist dismiss the mother's offer to provide medical information? Should she have asked for Lynn's medical records so that she could learn more about her new client? Let us look at the possible advantages and disadvantages of obtaining medical information.

A positive aspect of medical information is that therapists' fantasies about a client's condition, its cause and its prognosis can be minimised in the light of scientific facts. For example a client with a severe skin disorder may trigger an image of leprosy and fear of contamination. Such associations are not conducive to the therapeutic relationship. With some conditions, such as epilepsy, therapists need to know how to act when the client has seizure. In general, once therapists have been told by the client about her or his medical condition, and are then able to relate to the client's subjective experiences, they may seek further information and understanding of that condition through further reading. Information on the condition as such is different from information on the client.

On the other hand medical information can prove detrimental to the therapeutic relationship. For example, when a therapist is informed about a client's medical condition before meeting the client it is highly likely that the therapist's perception of the client's concerns will be distorted (see Chapter 5). Also, as mentioned above, possession of a description of the medical condition could trigger an unconscious fear of contamination, pain and death, which might cause the therapist, especially if this is her or his first disabled client, to defend against this fear by relating to the client as a 'case' rather than a fellow human being.

Any information on the client that is obtained from someone other then the client means introducing a third party into the relationship, and might divert the therapist's attention away from the client's concern towards the concerns of those who supply the information. Clients who realise that their therapist is using other sources of information about them may find it difficult to develop trust in the therapist, who coud be perceived as going behind their back. Although it is difficult at nes, therapists have to trust that their clients will tell them as much alhey need to know. The information is not always straightforward, anmay sometimes come in disguise, as happened in the following vignett

Nine-year-old Gill's speech and gait were affected by cebral palsy, and she had recently had several mild convulsive fits. Gi had been in therapy with me for nearly two years. One day she took aiece of card from her box, balanced it carefully on my head and saidStay still, relax.' She added: 'It will take only twenty minutes.' Shthan proceeded to put toys, pencils and more pieces of card on my hed, all the while issuing instructions. I was somewhat nonplussed ...

What was it all about, what was she trying to tell me? Hoever after a while it all fell into place. Through this game Gill was lling me what had happened to her at the hospital when the neurologi had been trying to find the cause of her fits. In this 'role play' Gill ws the doctor and I became the patient. She was trying to communica her feeling of puzzlement, of wondering what was going on. Taking n the role of a medical person was an attempt to understand the aspets of her experience that had not made sense to her at the time.

If Gill's mother had told me about this procedure beforehnd I would not have gone through the wondering, not-knowing phas and Gill would have been denied the opportunity to share her puzzlment and struggle with the unknown. Role-play with children, like cting out with adults, is a form of 'communication by impact' that allos the therapist a glimpse of the client's world. The role reversal helpe Gill to work through the experience of being subjected to the medica procedures, and of being just as out of control during the tests as sh was during her fits. Because of her age Gill did not have access to infrmation on the tests and therefore needed her therapist to share her fears and the experience of 'un-knowing'.

Although health professionals and their patients share the common aim of improving the health of the patient, conflicts can arise over certain medical procedures. For example procedure may improve a patient's physical health while at the same time reducing his or her overall quality of life. Furthermore some medical professionals overlook issues such as the patients' dignity and their ability to withstand pain, while patients do not always understand the reasons for their actions and therefore find it difficult to trust them.

Kate had muscular dystrophy, which affected her ability to move her arms. To slow down the process of muscle wastage it was important to keep her arms moving, so the physiotherapist instructed Kate's helpers not to assist her at meal times as feeding herself would provide good exercise for her arm muscles. Every time Kate's favourite meal – freshly fried fish and chips – was put in front of her she could see it and smell it, but by the time she managed to get it to her mouth it was cold and tasteless so she was never able to enjoy it. Furthermore the arduous and exhausting ordeal made her too tired to enjoy any other activity. Why was it not left to Kate to decide what was more important, after all she was the one who had to endure the consequences?

A psychotherapist working in an environment such as a hospital can be tempted to fall in with the medical team as this may feel safer and more comfortable than maintaining a separate position. But clients who perceive the therapist as part of the team, as 'yet another medic', may not be able to view the therapist as an ally and lose the opportunity for a relationship that is influenced by no perspectives other than their own.

Let us look again at Lynn's first words to her therapist: 'Sometimes I feel very upset, but I can't be upset at home, my parents don't like it. My mother is very worried about me; she would not allow me to dye my hair, like my cousin does. She says it is too dangerous; it may hurt my eyes.' On the surface Lynn is sharing with her therapist an aspect of her life at home, but in order to improve our understanding of her communication we need to ask why she chose this particular story. In this narrative Lynn paint's a picture of caring parents whose concern about her medical condition renders them unable to relate to her as a young woman – they can only see her illness. Perhaps one of the reasons for her unconscious choice of this narrative as her first communication was to tell her therapist that there were enough people worrying about her medical condition and she did not need the therapist to become one of them. What she needed was an ally who would not succumb to the anxiety provoked by her physical condition and would relate to her as a person. In time, as trust developed, Lynn came to speak to the therapist about her experience of and feelings about her condition.

Autonomy and external information

The provision and receipt of care can confuse self-perception and self-image because there is a distortion of the balance of power. In the patient – carer relationship the patient, due to his or her medical condition, has to hand over responsibility to the carer. Such a relationship is reminiscent of the early mother – baby relationship, where the mother has absolute responsibility for the care of her baby. A competent mother who is not too anxious can derive a great deal of satisfaction from having absolute power over another human being, and when a patient is in need of total care the same could be said of the competent carer. It is healthy and positive for the carer to derive satisfaction from the demanding task of providing such care. However the challenge is to let go of this power when the patient's need for total care subsides.

The intensity required to provide total care can lead carers to treat their patients as annexes of themselves; rather than as a separate entities. Disabled people who experience long periods of total care have to learn to tolerate a state of fusion with their carers, and may even long for it. The regressive experience of giving up responsibility can lead to a 'Peter Pan syndrome', whereby patients who have lost trust in their own body try to avoid regaining adult responsibility: in order to remain in the regressive state of total care.

When a client shows a tendency towards the Peter Pan syndrome the therapist's role is to identify and acknowledge the fear and exhaustion being experienced by the client. The client's need to retreat from the harsh reality of life should be respected by the therapist, while facilitating the process of restoring the client's autonomy. The first step in this process is to establish the separateness of each individual by defining the boundaries between self and others. One way of doing this is to insist that any information on an individual belongs to that individual and can be shared with others only at the individual's discretion. Therapists who follow this rule build up a relationship based on respect. Therefore the way in which medical or any other information on a client is to be managed must be carefully considered. Unless such information is essential to the therapy the therapist should refrain from seeking or accepting it prior to seeing the client. This will also help to prevent the therapist's perception of the client from becoming contaminated. The drawback of expecting clients to be the sole source of information is that they have to repeat their story yet again. However, most people are grateful for the opportunity to do so, especially if they can do it at their own pace. People do not often come across a listener who is genuinely trying to understand their unique experience, rather than comparing it with that of others in order to diagnose and categorise.

LEARNING POINT

- When psychotherapists minimise their exposure to their clients' medical information they enhance their ability to understand and work with the clients' own perceptions and experiences.

Managing the Therapeutic Frame

Home visits

The voice on the answerphone said 'This is Terry, social worker from team B. My client, Mrs Soyer, needs counselling. She is in her early seventies, very fragile and frightened.' The therapist returned the call and explained to Terry that standard procedures covered earlier. Mrs Soyer herself had to call the counselling centre to make an initial appointment. Terry was surprised: 'Can't you just tell me when you intend to go to see her and I'll arrange it.' The therapist realised that there was a discrepancy between the concept of counselling held by Terry, the well-meaning social worker, and the counselling she was there to provide. In the discussion that followed Terry explained that Mrs Soyer lived in a first-floor flat without a lift and that she had difficulty negotiating the stairs. She was also a little paranoid and very suspicious of strange people. Therefore it would be best if he went with the therapist to see Mrs Soyer in her own home, as she knew and trusted him.

Should the therapist have gone along with Terry's idea? Visiting the client at home would have been an opportunity to ascertain the extent of her physical limitations and emotional distress as well as offering a glimpse of her lifestyle and other pertinent factors. It would also have pleased the social worker. However the therapist explained to Terry that the time and place of the meeting had to be negotiated between herself and Mrs Soyer in accordance with the counselling service's policy, in which home visits were a rare exception. Terry reluctantly agreed to give Mrs Soyer the phone number, but warned that this would not work. Nonetheless Mrs Soyer did call, and a few days later went to see the therapist in the consultation room. She had also managed to arrange her own transport.

In the first session Mrs Soyer talked about certain doctors who had not listened properly to her description of her complaint, misdiagnosed her and administered an unnecessary treatment that had caused her a problem with balancing. In effect she was expressing distrust in the professionals' ability to understand her needs and respond to them appropriately. She perceived her disability as the result of the professionals' incompetence. Listening to all this the therapist asked herself the same questions that I had asked myself during my encounter with Gill. 'What is this all about?' and 'What is the client saying to me?' Before attempting to answer these questions we need to map out the context in which this first session took place.

- The idea to seek counselling had come from the social worker. Therefore counselling was perceived by the client as an element of social work provision.
- The social worker had promised to arrange it for her.
- The therapist had not cooperated with the social worker.

The therapist tried to organise her thinking around these facts and began to formulate an interpretation based on the mother–child relationship:

- The social worker and the therapist represented the parental couple getting together in order to take care of the client/child.
- The social worker represented an overprotective parental figure who offered help without considering or encouraging the clients real ability.
- There was a split in the parental couple and the client received a different message from each party. The social worker's message was 'You are weak, unable to go out; you need me to look after you', while the therapist's message was 'You are an adult and I will relate to you as such, unless you ask to be treated differently.'

The therapist's belief in Mrs Soyer's ability encouraged the latter to exercise her autonomy. However the conflict between the social worker and the therapist made her uneasy. Doctors, social workers and therapists were all professionals who were there to help her. Yet in her experience they did not always know what they were doing and could actually cause harm. Her first comment was an unconscious plea to the therapist to listen to her and not to misdiagnose her as the doctor and social worker had done. Another interpretation is that the therapist had misdiagnosed the client's ability and made a heavy demand on her by relating to her as an autonomous adult. The therapeutic relationship that followed this initial exchange indicates that the therapist's diagnosis was right – Mrs Soyer kept her regular counselling appointments for two years and arranged her own transport without the social worker's help.

'Why don't you see people in their own home?' This question has been put to me many times, mostly by social workers and other health and care professionals, and rarely by clients seeking the service. The issue of home visits is a delicate one and requires sensitive judgement. For some of those who seek professional help it is very difficult or even impossible to leave their home to meet in a neutral place, so home visits are the only way to receive necessary services, including psychotherapy. These people, however, represent only a small minority of those who are reluctant to leave their home. The majority, for variety of reasons, are unwilling to make the effort to go out but are well able to do so, although some support, night be needed. The difficult task for a professional helper is to differentiate between the two groups.

There is an innate conflict between autonomy and dependency. The wish to help and be needed, which often underlies people's decision to enter a choice caring profession, can at times promote dependency when the declared aim is to facilitate autonomy and self-reliance.

Imagine a scenario in which the therapist goes along with the social worker to see the client at home. A triad is created in which the social worker is in the paternal role. The therapist might then be perceived by the client as someone who cannot manage on his or her own. Being offered a 'weak' therapist could reinforce the client's sense of helplessness and diminished autonomy.

Another aspect of home visits is lack of neutrality. The home is the client's private space. The client may initially be keen for the therapist to enter and share this space, but as in most relationships there are likely to be times when the client needs to express his or her anger. For example when a therapist takes a break, some clients communicate their sense of abandonment and rejection by cancelling a session before or after a scheduled break. Clients who find the therapist's absence very painful may not even call to cancel as they need the therapist to experience anxiety and frustration. This is impossible when therapy takes place at the client's home as the only options are to call and cancel the session, to be out, or not to answer the door, none of which deliver the same emotional message as letting the therapist wait, not knowing whether the client will come. Other factors that can erode the privacy and neutrality of the therapeutic space include other people sharing the home, unexpected callers and telephone calls.

Therapy in the client's own home is a compromise. The home contains a range of memories and experiences that may need to be addressed from a distance. Whenever possible the therapist should offer clients uncompromised therapy. However if a client is unable to get to the consulting room the therapist may make an exception, but this has to be considered very carefully as home visits can create confusion and undermine the therapeutic relationship.

LEARNING POINTS

■ Therapists who work with disabled people may find themselves under pressure to offer therapy at a client's homes because of mobility or health problems.

- Most clients respond positively to therapy in a neutral environment, and can be encouraged to overcome the problem of getting there.
- Conducting therapy in a place that is not neutral, such as the client's home, is a compromise that should be avoided whenever possible.

Entering the consulting room

Like most of the issues discussed in this chapter, the management of boundaries is not peculiar to work with disabled people. However the existences of a disability and some habitual reactions can confuse the way in which responsibility is shared between client and therapist in the therapeutic relationship.

Let us look at how clients enter the consulting room. Ideally the client should arrive at the appointed time and the therapist should open the door. But when clients first have to wait in a waiting area, who shows them to the consulting room? Counsellors and psychotherapists working in the NHS or independent agencies are often expected to come out of the consulting room and escort the client into the room. This routine is similar to the way in which doctors or their nurse usher in patients, but is it really appropriate for a client in a psychotherapeutic relationship?

There are some fundamental differences between the nature of doctors' work and that of therapists. Doctors mainly operate on the basis of one-off appointments, while therapists aim to develop a regular, ongoing relationship. Also, in the course of their work doctors have to respond to emergencies and individual consultations often take longer than expected. Therefore patients have to wait until the doctor is available. In psychotherapy the clients have a fixed time, so, having to wait for the therapist to invite them in indicates that this time is not under their control but is dependent on the therapist's discretion or generosity. Such an arrangement could feed the clients' helplessness and dependency and delay autonomy. If possible clients should be encouraged to knock on the therapist's door at the appointed time. Unless the security arrangements in the building or a physical impairment necessitate it, escorting clients should be avoided because of its infantilising nature.

Clients who need to be escorted

Ian, a successful journalist in his mid thirties, was paralysed as a result of a train collision. His wheelchair was not motorised and he needed a carer to escort him to and from the therapy sessions. This arrangement put into question Ian's body boundaries. Had the wheelchair become an integral part of Ian, forming a single unit? And what about the carer? Had he or she been integrated into the entity called Ian? In general, if a wheelchair and carer are there to replace disfunctioning limbs, does this mean that they are perceived as part of the client's body? There is no absolute answer because each individual relates differently to his or her wheelchair and carer. At one end of the scale are those who view their wheelchair as part of their body self, at the other end are those who hate their wheelchair because it is a symbol of their dependency, and in the middle are those who see it just as a mechanical device that facilitates movement.

The therapist could become another element in this complex interplay of testing and reidentifying boundaries. When a client in a wheelchair is escorted the therapist needs to consider two additional issues: how to relate to the wheelchair, and how to relate to the escort.

The wheelchair

As a matter of course, it is the therapist's responsibility to arrange the consulting room furniture. The chairs should be close enough not to cause a sense of isolation, but sufficiently far apart to avoid the sense of suffocation that can result from close proximity. However clients in a wheelchair have the relative freedom to choose where to position themselves in the room, which can leave the therapist with a dilemma. Should they be left free to choose any position, or should they be guided to a position that the therapist believes to be conducive to therapy? What should the therapist do if a client positions him- or herself too near or too far away?

The question of whether to reposition the client is a delicate matter because a wheelchair is not just another piece of equipment. As discussed above, for some people it becomes part of their identity, even part of their body. Therefore the experience of being moved around in a wheelchair is comparable to a non-disabled person's experience of being pushed about.

One day Ian was wheeled by his escort into the consulting room and positioned so that the therapist could not close the door. The therapist said 'I will have to move you forward a bit so that I can close the door.' Ian did not respond immediately. Later on in the session he talked about old friends who were trying to keep in touch with him. He was unsure of their motives. Did they enjoy his company or did they wish to see him out of pity and charity? Ian was not only sharing his doubts about his friendships, he was also telling the therapist that the experience of being wheeled by her had harmed his fragile sense of equality as a fellow human being.

The escort

When a client comes with an escort the therapist has to consider carefully how to relate to the escort. Lynn's mother was an example of a pushy escort, and it was clear to the therapist that the therapeutic space had to be protected from invasion. Paradoxically an overinvolved and seemingly strong escort can help to sharpen the therapist's awareness of the need to maintain the therapeutic boundaries and ensure the client's privacy and confidentiality. Such an escort also frees the therapist from the need to look after him or her, so she can fully engage herself in her client's needs without feeling mean or guilty about neglecting the escort. It was different when Ian and his escort were late for therapy one day after a very difficult journey in a winter storm. The therapist's impulse as host was to offer the escort a warm welcome and a cup of tea. This friendly human gesture might have made the therapist feel good about herself and comforted the escort, but how would it have affected the client?

Therapists who work with escorted clients have to re-examine the therapeutic construct and consider the escort as a third party. Unless the escort is the client's partner and both come for couple or family therapy, the therapist should keep the interaction with the escort to the very minimum. But because the escort is a fellow human being and not an inanimate object it can be difficult to ignore his or her needs. Ian's therapist had to remind herself that the purpose of the journey was Ian's session and therefore she should leave the escort to take care of himself. Looking after the escort's needs would have taken away one of the fundamental elements of the therapeutic relationship: that for the duration of the session the client has the therapist entirely to him- or herself. Even with careful consideration and thoughtful action, the fact that an escort is involved in the relationship has a direct impact on the therapy and has to be integrated into the therapist's thinking and interventions.

Some readers may not see the practical issues discussed in this chapter as the main concern of psychotherapy. Yet having to acknowledge the particular reality of disabled people heightens therapists' awareness of the significance of the setting as part of the therapeutic frame (Langs, 1988), and highlights the importance of holding and

containment (Winnicott, 1975b) as fundamental elements of the therapeutic process.

LEARNING POINTS

- The need to consider and protect clients' autonomy increases in inverse proportion to their degree of physical dependency.
- When a client's life is affected by physical constraints the signifi-
cance of the therapy's practical and physical aspects increases.

IMPLICATIONS FOR THERAPISTS

Disability affects the therapeutic relationship in the following ways.
Psychotherapy with people who are in physical as well as emotional
distress can be a difficult and lonely experience. Unlike doctors and
nurses, who have the opportunity to discharge their anxieties through
action-oriented tasks, psychotherapists' task is to stay with distress and
anxiety to enable clients to gain a better understanding of their predicament, and thereby to restore or achieve autonomy. Therapists working
with people who are also under medical care may be consciously or
unconsciously tempted to alleviate difficult emotions by busying themselves with medical issues.

Therapists who find themselves in close proximity to what seems
like overwhelming human suffering sometimes develop distancing
defence mechanisms. Distancing techniques aim either to objectify the
other, for example by devising pseudoscientific, rigid assessment procedures, or to infantilise through a patronising attitude. Whatever the
distancing method the usual outcome is lack of respect for the client's
who are related to as though they are objects or a babies.

Working with disabled people adds a sense of urgency to the wish
to help, which can cause considerable frustration as therapists recognise their limitations. A difficult task for therapists is to identify and
monitor how differences in appearance and physical functioning affect
the way they relate to disabled people. For example if a person's
speech is unclear and garbled it might wrongly be assumed that the
thought process behind it is also unclear and garbled. Disabled people
are very sensitive to the attitudes prompted by the assumed link
between physical disability and mental impairment.

Summary

This chapter has focused on the clinical practice of therapeutic work with disabled people. The emotional and practical difficulties raised by clients' disabilities have been addressed in terms of management of the therapeutic setting and relationships with other caregivers. The challenge of maintaining neutrality and privacy has been contrasted with the temptation to allow third-party involvement. The main theme has been the importance of maintaining clear and firm boundaries when developing and strengthening the autonomy of disabled people.

THE WORLD OF A DISABLED CHILD: THE STORY OF JOE

Referral and Pretherapy Interaction

I first heard about Joe when his mother called me at the disability counselling service to discuss her concern about her disabled child. She was looking for someone who understood disability to help Joe improve his behaviour at school. She had been relieved to find an agency that offered counselling and psychotherapy to people affected by disability. I explained that the agency was mainly geared to working with adults, which meant that we did not have suitable premises for working with children, nor did we specialise in that area. Nonetheless she felt that our involvement and familiarity with disability would provide the missing element needed for Joe's development. After negotiating with Joe's school we agreed that I would see Joe at school for an initial session with a view to assessing his suitability for regular therapy.

The outcome of the assessment was that Joe had the potential to benefit from regular therapy, and that it might also be indirectly helpful to the school and Joe's family. All four parties involved – Joe, his mother, the head teacher and myself – agreed on a weekly session in the school premises. As the person responsible for Joe, Joe's mother was invited to meet me every three months so as to include her in the therapeutic process. The following account covers the first 18 months of my working relationship with Joe.

Building Trust

Seven-year-old Joe lived with his younger sister and mother in an estate on the edge of a small town. He attended a mainstream school that had a policy of integrating disabled and non-disabled children in the same learning environment. His big dark eyes were set in a plump face topped with a short crop of blond hair. His expression alternated between a cheeky smile and a sad, thoughtful gaze. His left arm was paralysed as a result of cerebral palsy and could not be used. Although his left leg was also paralysed he was able to use it as a prop to support his unsteady gait. His speech was slightly slurred and not always easy to understand.

My anticipation of this therapeutic relationship oscillated between excitement, curiosity and concern about the new experience of working with a child. While contemplating this adventure, thoughts and questions about possible distinctions between child and adult psychotherapy began to surface. One such thought stemmed from the fact that in Western society children are not considered fully responsible for their actions and are not expected to take full charge of their life. How would this affect the psychotherapeutic relationship? Should relating to a child be conducted differently from relating to an adult, and if so, how?

In our culture children are not perceived as fully autonomous beings but as extensions of their parents or guardians. In adult psychotherapy a fundamental objective is for the client to learn to manage the tension between separateness and dependence, thus acquiring a degree of autonomy. Yet children's capacity to manage this tension alters according to their developmental stage. Piaget (1977), the Swiss educationalist, distinguishes between the heteronomy (being subject to external laws) of infants and the autonomy (having their own laws) of adults. In psychoanalysis this distinction between infant dependence and adult independence corresponds approximately to the anal stage of Freud's psychosexual stages, where sphincter control marks the achievement of autonomy. What is the significance of these differences?

Melanie Klein (1932) emphasises the similarities rather than the differences between child and adult psychotherapy, and argues that the differences are purely a matter of technique and not of principle. This acts as a reminder that the task of the therapist is to try to understand the anxieties expressed directly and indirectly during the therapeutic relationship.

One reason for developing a different technique for therapy with children is the need to keep a balance between respect for the child's autonomy and the fact that the child has not yet reached its full developmental potential. Another factor to consider is that children tend to make less use of verbal association and more readily express themselves through play and other activities.

Body Image and the Disabled Child

The term 'body image' was coined by Brain and Head (1941) to describe the vibrant, internally constructed ensemble of experiences, the internal image and memory of one's body in space and time. According to Freud 'a person's body, and above all its surface is a place from which both external and internal perception may spring' (Freud, 1923, p. 25). Tyson and Tyson (1990, p. 325) define body image as 'the mental representation of the body that evolves gradually and is modified through growth, maturation, and development. It does not necessarily correspond to the objective body.'

The continual interplay between the objective body (the body as measured and perceived by others) and our own experience triggers the creation of the internal perception of our existence – our body image. This process also involves comparing the objective body with the idealised wished-for body. Most people would probably admit to a desire to improve certain aspects of their body, as evidenced by the growing demand for cosmetic surgery. In a study of the phantom limb phenomenon the American neurologist Ramachandran (1998) considers Anosognosia, a disorder in which people react to a limb's loss of function with complete denial. Anosognosia and the neural mechanisms that block unwanted information were identified almost a century ago, yet there have been very few attempts to explore the extent of the unconscious roots of such denial. I believe that the craving for an unblemished body is a manifestation of the attempt to deny or delay the finality and humiliation of death. An old or impaired body is an unwelcome reminder of our inevitable end and the medical profession has been invested with the task of protecting us from death, of keeping our bodies in as near perfect condition as possible. It follows, then, that the medical profession sees disability as an imperfection or abnormality that has to be 'cured'; that is, the body is a mechanism and disability is a defect that has to be put right by the medical mechanic. The medical approach involves a static, change-resistant perception of the body that can easily provoke fear of change or difference. It does not allways allow for the subjective experiences of the individual.

Making Assumptions about Disability

As Joe and I were settling down for our first session he waved his good arm in a dramatic fashion and said 'I want to find disabled all over

England.' 'You want to meet other disabled people like yourself', I asked? This seemed an innocent enough assumption. After all I had been asked to work with Joe as a psychotherapist specialising in disability and Joe's physical impairment was visible, therefore it was easy to conclude that he perceived himself as a disabled person.

Joe was not having any of this: 'How can you see that I am disabled?' He demanded to know what it was that had led me to such an assumption, and what else I could see. This was followed by an attempt to offer me some guidance. He picked up a map of Mexico and said. 'You can get lost in Mexico.' This was Joe's way of telling me that working with him would be like entering a foreign country. My question had revealed that I obviously needed to learn more but also that I needed to be careful about who guided me. If Joe and I were to find our way together then I had better let go of my dependency on outside sources such as parents and teachers, and get into the habit of listening to Joe rather than to them. Joe was suggesting that I follow his map for guidance.

The impact of a first meeting is of immense importance to all relationships and even more so to the therapeutic relationship. Let us try to imagine how Joe perceived this new person, the therapist, who had suddenly entered his life. He was told that a counsellor would be meeting with him so that he could tell her what was hurting him inside, and I believe that the context of disability was mentioned. I do not know what fantasies and expectations were triggered by this information, but based on our initial interaction I assume that he was somewhat disappointed. Instead of just listening to him I responded to perceptions and assumptions that did not stem directly from our relationship. My interpretation suggested that he was disabled and therefore wanted to be with other disabled people. But Joe did not want to be labelled as disabled. He wanted to be seen as a whole person. By revealing that I saw him as disabled I introduced a problematic image, an image that he did not wish to be identified with. Yet he did refer to disabled people, so what was it about?

Now that I know more about Joe's defence strategy I can see that he was expressing an omnipotence fantasy, which is one of the defences children tend to use to protect themselves against the anxiety provoked by fear of abandonment. Joe perceived his disability as causing anxiety to the people who cared for him. He desperately needed his parents and teachers to be free of anxiety so that they could function properly and look after him. The anxiety-provoking disability was a bad object that he projected onto 'the disabled of England'. Once the disability had been externalised he was ready to join forces with this 'disability therapist' and to imagine himself as the one who would help or save the disabled of England. At that early stage I had not yet earned sufficient trust for Joe to let go of his omnipotence and expose his vulnerability or weakness, which in part he associated with being disabled. Why did I do it, why did I label Joe? Perhaps part of the reason was linked to the therapeutic frame in which our work took place.

The Therapeutic Environment

Joe's school had designated the resource room as the venue for therapy. As Joe's psychotherapist I was seen as an extension of parental involvement and was treated as a tolerated foreign body. This confused status and the unfamiliar environment made it difficult to manage and maintain the therapeutic frame. Joe, however, needed the therapist to be in charge of the environment so that he could feel held in safety. The school, with its teachers, classmates and parental involvement, was far from the neutral environment required for therapy, especially as I was unfamiliar with the territory. Perhaps this was concealed in his comment 'You can get lost in Mexico', that Joe was actually saying, 'Not only is my internal world unknown to you but you also need a map of my external world.' I responded by saying, 'You were surprised that I saw you as disabled and then you told me I could get lost and gave me a map. I think you were also saying to me that I should only listen to you and be careful.' Joe was relieved that I had heeded his warning and admitted my fault, and that neither of us was hurt or damaged by my 'imperfection'. We formed an alliance, a common ground for communication was established, and we agreed to meet once a week for 50 minutes in the resource room. I had brought a large box with the label 'Joe's box' to serve as part of the therapeutic frame. The box, which contained paper, pencils, sellotape scissors, plastic human and animal figures, glove puppets, plasticine and a small bottle of water, was intended to offer a sense of privacy and autonomy in a room that was not usually dedicated to the purpose of therapy.

LEARNING POINT

- Therapists should not assume they know the way, they need to listen carefully to the client, even if he or she is only a child, otherwise they will get lost.

From Fantasy to Reality

Joe, like most disabled children, was denied many of the peer group experiences of non-disabled children. For instance he could not take part in games and other physical activities – he could not run or catch a ball. His mother protected him by keeping him indoors when he was not taking part in supervised activities. As a result of this semi-isolation Joe had not had the opportunity to develop the social skills required for relating freely with other children. Another obstacle was the heavy burden imposed by adults' concern about his future, as expressed in his struggle with writing.

My work with Joe can be divided into three themes, through which Joe expressed himself and engaged with me. They were brought into the sessions in the following order:

- The 'provider'.
- The 'inventor'.
- The struggle with the absent daddy

The first two themes were an attempt to deny his limitations by creating a parallel reality.

The provider

During the early stages of therapy Joe was engaged in a chivalrous fantasy of feeding and looking after significant people in his life. I believe that my misguided interpretation earlier, relating to him as a disabled person, triggered some of his omnipotence fantasy. In other words Joe's needy part was projected onto others while he assumed the role of protector and provider of food.

'I want to go out with Anna, I want her to come to my house and I will give her tea.' This comment seemed innocent enough and appropriate for a seven-year-old boy, but as the weeks went by it became clear that Anna never went to his house, giving him feeble excuses such as 'I need to go shopping.' Joe then decided to take action: 'I will write a letter to Anna's mummy, so she will bring her to my house.' Joe was in a mainstream school where most of his friends were able-bodied. His mother, like many mothers of disabled children, was very protective, which restricted free peer interaction. Therefore his experience of social interaction was mainly limited to adults. Therapy provided a setting where he could swap roles and play the adult's part.

At that time Joe's perception of the relationship between his parents was rather confused. 'My daddy does not love my mummy' he blurted out one day; and in the following session, 'I like mummy 'cause she gives me food.' Joe was aware of his dependence on his mother for survival and sensed that in order for her to be there for him she needed to be supported by his father, but if the father was not there to support her (I learnt later from his mother that her husband had left home by then) Joe was the only 'man' she could rely upon. This was both frightening and tantalisingly exciting for a seven-year-old boy, who was experiencing the Oedipal triadic wish to replace his same-sex rival. The guilt that follows this fantasy can turn into fear if the fantasy becomes reality, and having managed to get rid of his rival Joe was overwhelmed with a conflicting feeling of triumph on the one hand and fear of retaliation on the other, as well as grieving for the loss of his father.

The anxiety and sense of loss caused by the parental separation were unbearable. Joe told me about a dream he had had: 'I opened a box of Cornflakes – and inside were many hundred pounds.' He paused for a few minutes, reliving his dream, and than said: 'I know what to do with the money, I will get lots of Chinese food.' The theme of this dream was clearly linked to his wish to replace the absent father – Joe created an omnipotence fantasy in which he was filling the emptiness by being the provider of food. The foreignness of the food could have been a reference to the strangeness of having therapy with someone who had a foreign accent, touching upon the tension between belonging and being an outsider. The fact that the fantasy appeared in a dream indicates that Joe had begun to grapple with the reality principle. For a child of seven, being the provider can only belong to the world of dreams. In other words Joe was beginning to relinquish his omnipotence and his denial of reality.

In a later session I told Joe that a break in therapy was imminent. I had to bear in mind that a child's perception of time might be different from that of an adult, reflecting the child's experience of the world. The pace at which children's bodies change and develop, combined with their shorter time in the world, results in a more intense sense of time and a fear of separation. Winnicott (1988) argues that continuity and order are essential during early development and that the child is dependent on his mother/carer to provide these. In adult psychotherapy, breaks in the routine are often experienced as a reminder of limited control and the finiteness of life. Even a planned break can trigger confusion, loss of control and a sense of helplessness (Seligman, 1975). For children the disruption of a break also highlights their dependency and puts to the test the delicate process of developing trust in therapy as a process, and in the therapist as a reliable person.

Most children do not use a diary to manage their time – this is the responsibility of the adults in charge of them. A useful way of addressing breaks when working with a child is a therapy session chart, which in essence is a graphic representation of the forthcoming weeks that visually incorporate the break. The chart I made for Joe had a box for each therapy session and boxes with crosses for the dates representing the break. Joe did not like it. He pushed the chart aside, picked up the water bottle, put it under his paralysed arm and unscrewed the cap with his other hand. He took a sip of water and then stopped and looked around. He noticed the chart, pulled it nearer to him and then vigorously poured water over it. He suddenly stopped and said 'I want hot chocolate NOW! Please . . .' I replied, 'You want something nice and warm in your tummy – maybe you feel empty inside like the crossed boxes on the chart that will become empty when I am away so you were trying to feel with water.' Joe calmed down and wrote 'NOW' on a piece of paper. His anxiety about the break in therapy had been put into words. Understanding the link between the break and his desire for a comforting drink enabled his wish for immediate gratification to be sublimated into writing, a 'civilised' activity, as Freud (1911) put it. This created a thinking space in which the frustration of the delay could be tolerated. Bion (1962, p. 112) explains that the 'Inability to tolerate frustration can obstruct the development of thoughts and a capacity to think.'

At the beginning of the new school year Joe said 'I want to ask Miss M [his new teacher] to come with me to the pub in the evening. No, not to the pub, somewhere where they give you food'. It seems that in the process of shaping his idea some transformation took place. Through verbalising and expressing his thoughts Joe was able to let go of the dubious aspect of his omnipotence fantasy of 'male in a pub' and turn it into a wish to feed and be fed.

Just before coming to see Joe that day I had found out that I would have to miss two meetings. When I told Joe he became very angry and painted all over the table and other furniture, as well as throwing objects around the room. I told him that I knew he was angry with me because I had had a break not that long ago and this was too much. Providing an emotional rationale for his behaviour enabled him to express his feelings plaintively in words: 'Don't go, why do you want to go, what will you do, whom will you see?' At the end of the session he was playing with glove puppets when he said, 'You will be Miss M [his teacher] and I'll eat you.' Anticipating the abandonment of yet another break, Joe was expressing a wish to incorporate a parental figure inside his body and thus avoid separation. Furthermore the combination of therapist and teacher seemed to offer the desired strength. Playing, rather then pretending, was another small step towards letting go of his omnipotence fantasy of being a grown-up man in a pub and allowing himself to be more of a playful child.

LEARNING POINT

■ When working with children, dealing with breaks inevitably involves addressing their capacity to appreciate, or to deny, the passing of time, as well as their way of managing separation.

Joe seemed to have received and internalised a message that being a small disabled boy was unsafe. Where could such a message have come from? Winnicott (1971, p. 131) describes the process by which infants discover how they are being perceived by the primary care-giver/mother: 'what does the baby see when he or she looks at the mother's face? I am suggesting that ordinarily, what the baby sees is himself or herself.' The mother's role of mirroring gives back to the baby the baby's own self. What, then, may occur when the mother is confronted with a damaged or sick baby? When anxiety and perhaps guilt are the dominant emotions felt by the mother, what will the baby see in the mother's face? Although there is no way of knowing conclusively what babies think and feel, observational studies such as those conducted by Winnicott (1958), Mahler et al. (1975), Stern (1985) and many others suggest that babies believe that they are the cause of the anxiety communicated through the mother's face. When the mother is worried about her child the mirror in her eyes tells the baby that something is wrong. Lussier (1980) suggests that the mother's interpretation of her child's damaged body could become a castration threat or stir up a threat of ego disintegration through the loss of a body part. Then the child will not be a mirror for the mother and the mother will not be a mirror for the child. Rather the child will learn to relate to his or her body in the way the mother once related to it. This illustrates the precariousness of the psychoemotional position of the disabled child.

Kohut's (1977) description of the role of infantile grandiosity in the developmental process offers a useful model for understanding Joe's way of expressing his omnipotence. Kohut argues that during the course of optimal development the grandiose, exhibitionistic self-image becomes connected to a 'self-object' (parental figures). The infant perceive itself as perfect and therefore admired. In turn the image of the self becomes fused with the idealised parental figure, which is seen as perfect, and the infant is part of it. But Joe was not able to idealise a parental figure, and was therefore trying to turn himself into one. Stern (1985) compares the traditional psychoanalytic view to that stated by Kohut and the self-psychologists. Stern concludes that there is a lifelong need for a self-object; that is, the reality of one person using some aspects of another person as a functional part of the self to provide a stablising structure against fragmentation. The need for a self-object continues throughout life and is not phase specific. This view is particularly useful for appreciating the way in which disabled people can reach maturity despite the fact that their physical differences prevent them from going through the traditional development and psychosexual stages.

According to Joe's mother, his father found it difficult to relate to his disabled son. He tended to ignore or dismiss him while giving affectionate attention to his non-disabled daughter. Although the mother's assertion cannot be validated we can assume that Joe perceived that his father was not proud of him. According to Kohut (1966, p. 252) 'the child needs the gleam in the mother's eye in order to maintain the narcissistic libidinal suffusion which now concerns . . . the function and activities of the various maturational phases'. Joe did not see a gleam in his father's eye, he was not admired because he was not perfect. Did this imperfection drive his father away?

The above material indicates that Joe was trying to heal his narcissistic wound by assuming the role of the father. Perhaps he was also trying to create the good father he needed but could not find.

Having realised that breaks meant only temporary separation, Joe no longer felt that he had to feed the adult he was dependent upon, or hold her in his tummy in order to survive. His separation anxiety had subsided. He turned his attention to Danny, a classmate who used a wheelchair: 'I want to take him to a fish and chip shop to buy some chips for him and for me.' Although Joe now trusted that I would not disappear he still needed an omnipotence fantasy to sustain his psychic reality while I was away. In the absence of any available good objects he turned to the fantasy of himself as provider. Danny, who was the only other disabled child in his class, was a wheelchair user and Joe saw himself as non-disabled in comparison.

During a session three weeks after the break, Joe was looking for the bottle of water that was usually present in his box. When he could not find it he became angry and stuck sellotape over my mouth, saying 'Don't talk! Keep your mouth closed'. When I hummed to indicate compliance he said 'Don't hum, be quiet!' While he was busy gagging me he said '1993 you were born, I will hit you', then he picked a stick from the shelf and started to hit me (Joe was born in 1993). Still gagged, I took the stick from him and placed it back on the shelf. Joe did not resist. He kept telling me to be quiet, and then said 'You will die.' He picked up the stick again, and once again I took it away.

Being helped to control his aggressive impulses seemed to come as a relief. Joe was pleased and took off the gag, saying 'You can talk now, you will be good.' He then engaged in an attempt to write a 'book'. Joe's writing did not match his developmental age, he had yet to make friends with pen and paper: 'I cannot tell this to my parents they will be mad at me, I hate to write, it takes me a long time, but I have to do it because I need to get a good job.' At the end of the session he refused to leave the therapy room. In response to my comment 'We will be here again next week', he replied 'It will be too late.'

Joe had experienced my neglect to bring the bottle as an attack on the newly born Joe in 1993, so I had become the baby and Joe the cruel parent. He had needed me to know how it felt to be helpless and frightened. He had been trying to 'kill' the helpless baby, which had been projected onto me. I had been both the baby and the therapist/mummy who forgot to feed her baby. This carelessness meant the baby would die, so mummy should do likewise. When I had prevented him from 'killing' me by putting away the stick he had been relieved to be saved from his own self-destruction. Yet in Joe's world it was still too dangerous to be little if you were imperfect. Having survived the attack on me and on himself, Joe had turned his attention to the grown-up world of book writing. This had been difficult for him as his paralysed arm made writing a lengthy and arduous task. He had been forcing his damaged body to compete in a hostile world.

When we met again two weeks later Joe was with his helper, and for the first time in our relationship he was reluctant to come with me. For a moment he seemed confused and bewildered, then a sudden change occurred and the clinging, withdrawn child became bouncy and happy, glad to walk with me to the therapy room. What was this sudden change about? The answer probably lies in the change to the therapeutic frame. Due to communication problems I had not known of the half-term break when I said in our last session 'I will be here next week'. During that session Joe had attacked me and told me that I would die, and although I obviously survived I had not come back when I said I would, which could have led him to believe that his attack had destroyed me after all. Therefore seeing me threw him into confusion; it was as if for a moment he thought I had come back from the dead.

From then on the water bottle became a vital element in our relationship. Frequently Joe reached for it, sucked on its neck and then squirted me with water. The bottle and its content had been given the double role of aggressor and feeder/comforter. When Joe had had enough experience to be confident about our ability to survive these attacks he was ready to move to a new stage, which was characterised by creating an 'invention'.

The 'inventor' – an attempt to create and control the desired environment

As the 'provider' Joe communicated his fear of abandonment as the rejected child. He was a little boy attempting to nurture himself and others in order to survive what he saw as a world of disfunctioning adults who were supposed to care for him but were failing to do so, including the therapist who was not there when expected. The only way to secure the mothering he wished for and needed was to provide it himself.

The omnipotence fantasy led to a perception of a mother who was weak and poor. Yet there was a part of Joe that acknowledged the need for adults, so he wished to support his mother/therapist as a way of ensuring his own survival. At the same time her perceived weakness was a source of guilt and fear of punishment. Joe seemed to be trapped in a cycle of attack – guilt – omnipotence. Being disabled, and in particular having to endure invasive treatment such as operations and other aggressive medical interventions, contributed to his feeling of helplessness and being attacked. Omnipotence fantasy was Joe's way of managing unbearable guilt, punishment, anxiety and frustration. The guilt was an outcome of his effort to make sense of and answer unanswerable questions: 'Why am I disabled?', 'Why am I different from my sister and other children?' Perhaps he had done something bad and was being punished? To escape from this dangerous place and haunting thoughts, Joe tried to create a world with different rules, a world where he was in charge.

Joe may have felt that his parents had failed him: they had not been able to provide him with a well-functioning body. Experiencing the parental couple as inadequate may have exacerbated his confusion, his fear of and anger towards these damaging adults. If they were there to protect him, why had they not prevented him from being damaged? Was it because they had been unable to prevent someone bad from harming him? If this had been the case it could happen again.

I believe that experiencing an intimate relationship with a therapist who evoked a mother but was not the mother created a space for Joe to work through his confusion and ambiguity about significant others. His anger towards and frustration about these 'useless' adults were manifested in his attempt to destroy the therapist/mother. The fact that I survived this attack strengthened the therapeutic alliance, and Joe now felt safe enough to explore his identity, particularly his masculinity.

Anna, the girl who had rejected him, came back on the scene: 'I want to change Anna to a man, I hate her, I want everyone to laugh at her.' (At the time Joe was busy making a box out of pieces of cardboard and was instructing me to sellotape them together.) He then added, 'I want to put the box over Anna, I want to hide my body from Anna.' He insisted on returning to his classroom with the box on his head. My interpretation and other tactics could not induce him to change his mind, so I ended up leading him along the school corridor, feeling embarrassed and professionally disabled. This experience offered me a momentary glimpse into Joe's unrelenting reality of difference and embarrassment.

At this point it is useful to address the way in which the separation of self and others can be confused with gender identity and body image. Freud's assertion that 'anatomy is destiny' implies that a sense of maleness is guaranteed by the possession of a penis (Freud, 1924, p. 178). This does not take into account the large range of cases where biological fact does not match felt gender identity, for example in transsexualism. Greenson (1968) argues that a boy's identification with his primary love object (his mother) may undermine his sense of masculinity, so he must dissociate himself from his mother if he is to form a secure masculine sense of self. Therefore Stoller's (1985) statement that a secure sense of masculinity is an achievement seems to suggest that gender identity is the outcome of a process rather than a biological given, and allows for differences in male self-image.

For Joe the box was a piece of armour that he invented to hide behind, whilst at the same time exaggerating his difference and impairment by putting it on his head and insisting on entering his class like that. This time he was doing it out of choice, he was taking control. The impaired body he had been given was hidden behind a grotesque body part of his own creation. When all else failed, frightening Anna was the only way to be noticed, to exist.

During the next session Joe sprayed water over me. He then posed, looked at me and said 'You are leaking'. 'Yes', I said, 'you have sprayed me and I am leaking because I cannot hold the water. Maybe you are also talking about last week when I could not hold the box inside the room and taking it outside felt like something leaked out of the room.' This interpretation seemed to make sense to Joe; he relaxed, sang and played for a while and then came to me and pressed his back against my side, as if wanting to get inside me. By allowing the box to be taken outside the therapy room I had become the weak and inadequate parent who could not hold or protect. Joe had perceived me as 'leaking'. Yet taking responsibility for my shortcomings had rectified some of the damage. The frame had become safe enough for Joe to wish he were inside me, where he could think and regain strength, as well as satisfy his curiosity and ensure that the leak had been mended from within.

After the long Christmas break Joe said 'I was very sad when you were gone, I am upset.' Later on in the session he said 'I want to make an aeroplane and I want to go to Spain with you, it will be very good.' Joe busied himself with making an aeroplane so that he could take his family to Spain, 'where all will be happy ever after . . . we'll all be safe inside'. I suggested that Joe wanted to be the good daddy, 'Yes', said Joe, 'I am daddy, I look after my family.' The aeroplane was growing, I was instructed to sellotape on more and more pieces of card and wheels. Joe was proud of it: 'It is my invention, this aeroplane.' He wanted to take it home and when I said that it belonged in our room Joe became very angry: 'I will take the sellotape, you will not stop me I will look after my children!' In the next session we made more wheels and the aeroplane was heading towards Switzerland to find Father Christmas. The omnipotence fantasy of being the absent father had given way to a search for a fairy tale daddy.

It was getting near Easter so we talked about the coming break and made a new chart. Joe grew a little upset and said he wanted to go on holiday and take me with him. He picked up the roll of sellotape, put it on my head and said 'You are the king'. We made more wheels and then he asked for a black pen, with which he wrote the word 'power' on a piece of card and stuck it onto the plane: 'I need to give it power so it can fly up and take us on holiday.' Joe was trying to create a parallel reality; he was defending against his separation anxiety by means of a fantasy in which the separating break was turned into a holiday together.

After the Easter break we had to move to another room due to a reorganisation at the school. Joe talked about his family finances. His mother did not know what to do, she had an overdraft and he wanted to give her money. 'Like a daddy', I said. 'Yes, I want to make a money-making machine, I want to be a king.' Joe than pretended to be a magician and made a money machine from card. He was disappointed when it failed to produce money – fantasy and reality were intertwined. His next money-making plan was to make sweets for adults to buy for their children. At the end of the session he was making a box in which to save money for a Chinese meal.

Yet again the adults responsible for his care had proved unreliable; his mother was in financial difficulty, his therapist had been away for three weeks, and the school had changed our room. It is very frightening to live in a world that is ruled by adults who are either not coping or unavailable, so he had summoned the king and the magician to rescue everyone. The fantasy had created a space in which to deal with the harsh reality of a bank overdraft and an unavailable therapist. He had let his imagination roam free, exploring new dimensions of coping in this chaotic world. During the next session Joe picked up the chart and asked me to draw 'happy faces' on the boxes representing future sessions and 'sad faces' on those representing missed sessions.

LEARNING POINTS

■ Creating space for fantasy alongside reality gives us an opportunity to express our wishes and aspirations and to feel in control.
■ Joe's fantasies were of a different kind. He was not pretending to be a provider, he was not playing make believe. Rather he felt the need to become a provider because he thought there was no other.
■ When reality and fantasy intertwine rather then exist alongside each other it can cause a confused perception of self and difficulty with relating to others.

The struggle with the absent father

The absence of Joe's father had been raised in the context of his mother's shortage of money. Joe's anxiety appeared to be growing – he asked me to see his mother and then his father. Chaos was reigning and Joe wished to reunite all the elements of his shattered world. I said 'You feel that mummy and daddy are not able to look after you, and you want me to help them, but if I do so I will not be your special person any more.' I was referring to my unique position as an ally who was independent of Joe's care and educational support system. Joe shouted 'You do what I tell you, you must give me the money . . .' He then kissed my cheek and walked away. He was thanking me for not letting his real parents into our relationship, for keeping his 'therapy space' free from interruption and making it safe to explore his internal world. At the end of the session he refused to leave the room. I ended up lifting him off the treatment bed, at which point he said 'You are a strong mummy'.

During the following session Joe tried to feed me with the water bottle. I suggested that he wanted to look after me in the same way as he was trying to look after his mother. A little while later he declared 'I am not disabled, I am independent.' Joe's disability made him dependent on others, but this was scary for a boy who experienced others as undependable. So denial of his disability seemed to be his only defence against the anxiety provoked by his unresolved identity conflict.

In the next few sessions Joe talked about his 'evil daddy' and asked me to 'sort him out'. Realising that this was not a realistic option, he said 'I don't want to have any memory of my daddy, this means I want to forget him.' At the end of the session he complained that meeting once a week was not enough, he wanted me to be there every day. We were approaching the long summer break and my forthcoming absence was turning me into the evil father, who was threatened with oblivion.

The sessions preceding the break focused on Ruth, his father's girlfriend. Joe began to test the boundaries, trying to start the session in the corridor but expressing relief when I told him that we had to talk in the room. Once we were in the room Joe said he wanted to have Ruth for himself, to 'break the couple' with the aim of winning the female. He then talked about his weekend with his father. They had gone to Ruth's house but Ruth had not approved of Joe's behaviour: 'She chucked me out of the front door and told me to wait outside.' He had found the experience of being reprimanded and punished by Ruth somewhat confusing: 'My Daddy show her to be nasty to me, I did say sorry and she still was nasty to me and shut me out of the door. It is too difficult, you need to talk to my Mummy.' I pointed out the parallel between the relationship with Ruth and the therapy: 'It is a little bit like here – you are in the room with me and at the end of the time I tell you to go, even when you don't want to go. It leaves you not knowing if I am a good Shula or a bad one.' Joe grew thoughtful: 'OK, yes I like Ruth. My Daddy does not deserve her, I want to make a real big bicycle to take Ruth on.' It seems that my interpretation, which had made Joe aware of the passing of time and the inevitability of the summer break, had prompted a flight into the omnipotence Oedipal fantasy of fighting his father and stealing Ruth.

Joe now moved away from his cardboard invention towards a 'real' and 'big' bicycle. In his desperation to understand and make sense of the conflicts between his internal experiences and the outside world, and because he thought he was seen as a disabled, damaged little boy, he felt he had to resort to 'propping' himself if he was to be loved and valued. He tried to compensate for his damaged limbs by creating an artificial ancillary to his body in the form of inventions or a bicycle.

Joe's father was not an easy role model. He was like a puzzle that needed to be put together. Joe knew that (a) his mother had 'chucked daddy out of the house' and (b) his father was a male. Were the two connected? When Ruth had 'chucked [Joe] out of the front door' he had believed this to be a common aspect of being a male. Therefore if you are a male you need somehow to please or manipulate females, otherwise you will be thrown out. But when you are little and disabled as well as a male it is so much more difficult.

During the sessions I was sometimes seen as a daddy, and when I was firm with Joe he said I was a 'hard daddy'. Tyson and Tyson (1990) suggest that consolation as well as fortification is found in idealisation and identification with various aspects of parents of the same sex. Joe experienced conflicting emotions towards his father. When he said 'Daddy is messing my head, he is not good for me' he was blaming his father for his difficulties and perhaps for his disability. Yet at a subsequent session he repeatedly said: 'I miss my Daddy'. This session took place on a Friday rather then the usual Monday. Perhaps Joe was missing the regularity and firmness of the frame, which he associated with 'daddy'. In light of his ambivalence about his father there could be no surprise about the following interaction, which conveyed Joe's anxiety about his mother not having a daddy to protect her.

Joe poured water over me and then angrily stepped on the empty plastic bottle and squashed it. With the bottle lying damaged on the floor, Joe asked 'Why I am disabled? What is disabled? I want more information.' The attack on the bottle could be seen as a metaphoric attack on the breast, demonstrating the extent to which he perceived his own aggression as dangerous and harmful. If the breast/bottle/parent is empty and damaged, then it follows that the baby will be damaged. There may be feeling of retaliation. Moreover there is now a vicious cycle: the 'good breast' is dependent on a mother being supported by a father. The lack of a good father renders mother a damaged breast. Joe, who was dependent on his mother, felt that the damaged breast was damaging him and was acting out his anger towards the damaged, disabling breast. In order to do so he had to feel that the therapy process was safe. Acting out his anger and surviving it facilitated his ability to think about himself as a disabled person who was ready to digest more information about disability.

Therapy offered Joe a trial run in which to experience the conflicting emotions of love, hate and guilt towards his father. Through the transference he was struggling with the fear of being abandoned and rejected by the therapist following his painful separation from his father.

Summary

Omnipotence fantasy was the main defence mechanism used by Joe throughout the three phases of the therapeutic relationship. Winnicott (1958, p. 130) argues that 'Omnipotent fantasies are not so much the inner reality itself as a defence against acceptance of it.' Joe experienced himself as different from others in a way that left him weak and dependent. This was a lonely and frightening place, from which he escaped by creating a parallel reality in which he played the role of a strong person who was in control and able to help others in the way he himself wished to be helped.

Our task in therapy was to find a way for him to differentiate between fantasy and reality. He had to learn to accept the pain and frustration of his internal and external reality, while keeping a separate space for play and fantasy. The comparatively safe and private therapeutic environment offered him a space in which to replay confusing and disturbing experiences so that he could learn to face and accept the fears, anxieties and joys of being a growing boy.

IMPLICATIONS FOR THERAPISTS

- Therapy cannot compensate for what is missing in a young client's life.
- Rather it offers an opportunity to experience a relationship that is unique in its neutrality, and thus differs from relationships with other adults such as teachers and parents.
- In order to achieve the essential separateness the therapist must refrain from direct involvement with childcare tasks.
- A child who is not dependent on the therapist for her or his everyday needs is able to explore the entire emotional spectrum in the safety of a therapeutic space that is removed from the chaos and turbulence of life.

Epilogue

In Joe's latest school progress review his teachers and support staff report that he no longer has tantrums and there has been a marked improvement in his academic achievements, especially in maths. Joe has found a way to relate to his environment as a place where adults can be trusted despite their occasional incompetence. Internalising the experience of a place where anger and other difficult emotions can be expressed and understood, rather than punished, has enabled Joe to tolerate his frustrations and respond better to the demands made of him at school and at home. Therapy offered him a place in which his confusion and frustration could be acted out and given a name. Joe has now started the process of letting go of the little adult and allowing the little boy to become a child among other children.

5

COMMUNICATION AND AUTONOMY

In order to live in the world of the non-disabled, many disabled people have to 'extend' their body, that is, to use an extraneous object to compensate for the missing element of their body, such as guide dogs for the blind and wheelchairs for people whose legs do not function. In recent years computer technology has opened a whole range of possibilities for disabled people. One area in which computers have made a significant impact on the life of some disabled people is communications technology. People who are able to hear and understand but are unable to produce speech can now express themselves verbally by means of an artificially produced voice. They can be heard, and hopefully understood, by others. The psychological effects of such communication have yet to be investigated. However, for psychotherapy, for which verbal communication is the main tool, communications technology is of particular interest as it has opened new possibilities in work with speech-impaired individuals.

In the following section the role of communications technology extension will be explored, addressing questions such as:

- What is being supplemented by the extension?
- What are the psychological implications of an extension?
- What does impaired communication mean to those who are affected?
- How does the development of communications technology affects the therapeutic relationship?

The Effect of Impaired Speech

Lorna was one of the first disabled people I met in my job as a social worker. She was a young woman in a wheelchair and wore a large bib to soak up her dribble. Spasms and other involuntary movements prevented controlled use of her hands, which meant that she was dependent on others for feeding, toileting, washing, dressing and all the other physical needs she had. Her speech was quite slurred and difficult to understand. Feeling out of control because of my inability to communicate with Lorna, I reverted to 'demand and control mode'; that is, I started to ask questions, one of which was, 'If by magic you could be granted one thing, what would it be?' I was expecting her to wish for the ability to walk or use her hands, but what Lorna wanted was clear speech. I was surprised by this as I had not thought that impaired communication would be experienced by people with multiple disabilities as the worst aspect of their condition.

Elizabeth Greeley (1996, p. 97), in her moving autobiography, writes: 'The part of my disability which causes me the most frustration is the way my speech and swallowing have been, and are, affected. This means that both communication through speech and socialising while having a meal are harder to carry out. In the past I have been very depressed about it: Not being able to communicate means isolation and frustration. Inflicting isolation and frustration on others, in the form of imprisonment and solitary confinement, is the most common method of punishment. Dostoevsky's experience of penal servitude, as related by Storr (1997, p. 59), permanently affected his view of human nature. Seeing convicts who for years had been ruthlessly crushed suddenly break out and assert their personality, often in a violent and irrational fashion, made him realise that individual self-expression or self-realisation was a basic human need. Dostoevsky observed people who had been silenced by their environment. They did possess the physical ability to speak and express themselves, but their physical survival depended on suppression of self-expression. Yet as Dostoevsky observed, there is a point at which life loses its value in the absence of self-expression. People with impaired speech are limited in the ways they can assert their personality. Freud relates Hans Sperber's (1912) hypothesis about the origin of speech. According to Sperber, speech originally served to summon the speaker's sexual partner (Freud, 1916, p. 201). If that is so, how do people without speech summon their sexual partner? What is the nature of communication when speech is absent or impaired?

Reactions to impaired speech

Through the story of Di we can gain an understanding of the way in which client and therapist react to impaired speech; how anxiety is evoked by the inability to interact in the direct vocal fashion to which therapists are accustomed. The hypothesis is that a client's impaired speech heightens the therapist's anxiety because it leaves the therapeutic dyad bereft of the protective cover of language, which as well as being a means of communication and interaction also offers defence options. It can hide thoughts and feelings as well as reveal them.

Young (1994), when discussing the problem of communicating the content of fantasies, quotes Riviere's concerns: 'they are apt to produce a strong impression of unreality and untruth' (Riviere, 1952, p. 20). In his commentary Young points to the elusive and subjective nature of the individual's inner world: 'This is because when we write or speak about phantasies we are clothing preverbal and very primitive mental processes in the language of words in dictionaries' (Young, 1994, p. 80). If we take Young's metaphor of language as clothing a step further, the body that clothes are supposed to protect could represent the raw internal world of both client and therapist. When language is absent or impaired, therapists may feel naked and exposed and grow anxious. They are deprived of the protective mechanism by which they manage and express their own and their clients' raw internal processes. Without the control offered by language the raw unconscious world holds the possibility of chaos and the eruption of fantasies. The therapist's experience could be compared to that of autistic people, who feel bombarded with anxiety provoking, unexplainable messages.

Donna Williams (1992, p. 182), who is autistic, relates her thoughts on the matter: 'for language to have any meaning one must be able to relate to it. For me, when the directness of relating is too great, the walls go up.' In a similar fashion, communicating with a client without the mediation of clear vocal speech can take away the therapist's 'protective clothing' and may feel too direct. This can lead to the therapist letting 'the walls go up' by allowing defences to take over.

LEARNING POINT

■ When speech is impaired, both client and therapist have to struggle to express and understand without the protective clothing of words.

The therapeutic frame

The following case study focuses on the paradox of the psychotherapeutic frame as both causing and containing anxiety. Marion

Milner (1950, p. 157) likens the therapeutic frame to that surrounding a work of art:

> Frames can be thought of both in time and in space. . . . When there is a frame it surely serves to indicate that what's inside the frame has to be interpreted in a different way from what is outside it. The frame marks off an area within which what is perceived has to be taken symbolically, while what is outside the frame is taken literally.

Milner describes the frame as a device for marking the boundaries between the inside and the outside. In the context of art the frame marks the boundary between the subjective reality of the artist's creation and what is taken as the objective reality outside this boundary.

When engaging within a framed space we enjoy the luxury of uninterrupted focusing in an environment protected from outside intrusion, in art as in therapy. By agreeing to adhere to certain ground rules the therapeutic dyad is defining the way in which the encounter will be managed. These ground rules are as follows: the therapy should be private, confidential and take place in a fixed location at a fixed time for a fixed length of time, and when applicable a fixed fee should be agreed. These ground rules regulate space, time and third-party involvement. When the ground rules are not upheld, due either to outside pressure on the therapist or to the therapist's own anxiety, it can, as will be seen in the following example, undermine trust in the therapist and the process.

LEARNING POINT

■ Most clients' comments and narratives contain references to the therapist's success or failure in maintaining a secure frame through an appropriate set of ground rules.

Di: The Young Woman Who Could Not Speak

Twenty-three year-old Di was living in sheltered accommodation in a small town. She had her own room and a key worker who helped with her daily needs. She was born with cerebral palsy and had limited control over her body. She was able to operate an electric wheelchair and a specially adapted computer with her left hand. The computer was operated by a wrist-switch fastened to the palm of her hand and pressed by her fingers. For all other physical functions she was entirely dependent on others.

Di attended a day centre that offered a variety of services to disabled people, one of which was counselling. When Di asked for counselling she was referred to me by her key worker at the day centre. Before I met Di the centre's occupational therapist approached me to say that she would set up Di's computer in the counselling room. She went on to explain that Di would not be able to communicate without the computer. This interaction with the occupational therapist made me anxious about Di before I had even met her.

The first session was a trial for both of us. I was anxious about communicating with a client who could not produce clear vocal sounds. The presence of the computer disturbed me because in general I did not feel at ease with machines. It reminded me of the cubists paintings by Braque and Picasso, where the body is separated into its constituent parts and scattered all over the canvas. Di's metaphoric mouth was on the table, separated from her body. She was able to produce sounds when she tried to speak, but they rarely resembled words. She was able to indicate 'Yes' and 'No'.

Everything that could go wrong did go wrong. It took Di quite a while and probably a great deal of frustration to manoeuvre the electric wheelchair into the small consulting room. Then the wire came off her wrist-switch. I started to feel somewhat unsure and Di became anxious, it did not fill safe. She asked for the occupational therapist and her key worker. The containment and support I was offering her was obviously not what she needed at the time. Yet I refrained from calling for help, and a few minutes later I managed to gather my thoughts and to talk to her about the difficulties being experienced by both of us. Di calmed down and presented a few typed pages. I was still too anxious to decode or interpret the message in Di's action; instead I read the typed message, holding on to the straw that was being offered. While I was reading Di tried to speak. After several attempts I thought I heard the words. 'I want to talk to you.' When I repeated them Di indicated 'Yes'. Then she typed 'I never want to see Nick again.'

Her relationship with Nick was the main issue in the typed pages. He had promised Di that they would get married, but his parents had not approved. Di was unconsciously reminded of her angry feelings about Nick by her disappointment at the way I was managing the session. Like Nick, who had promised to love her but then left, I had promised to help her and then it transpired that I could not even help myself. I said as much to Di. At the end of the session she typed 'Will you help me?' What made Di feel that despite my inadequacies I might be of help to her? Perhaps she was able to tolerate my bewildered reactions because as a veteran of disability she was used to people reacting to her with some degree of bewilderment.

The first step towards building trust had been to resist the temptation to call for help. The next had been to acknowledge my shortcomings and focus on listening and decoding Di's messages. So enough trust had been created for Di to want to see me again. We agreed to meet for a 50-minute session once a week on the same day at the same time in a quiet side room at the day centre.

Allowing a third party into a dyad can unbalance and disturb most relationships. In any dyad, a partner who shares experiences and information with a third party compromises privacy and confidentiality and risks the erosion of trust. However when a client, the therapist or both are unsure about the therapist's ability to function, as happened at my first meeting with Di, involving a third party can momentarily calm the tension and reduce anxiety. But there is a price to be paid: the development of trust is slower and the therapist is seen as less dependable. The temptation to involve a third party is particularly strong when working with disabled people who are dependent on the participation of others in the most intimate aspects of their lives. Therefore after the preliminary liaison with the key worker and the occupational therapist I refrained from looking at Di's file or discussing her with any other professional involved in her care. All that I learnt about Di came directly from her.

You may ask yourself, why deny the client and the therapist the possibility of help and support? Indeed the therapist should call upon others if that will serve to enhance the therapeutic relationship. For example, when working with a child the trust and sense of security of the child, who is not yet an autonomous person, is enhanced by the fact that the adults in charge of her or his care are working together. Yet the disabled adult's autonomy is often fragile and needs to be respected by the therapist. At the same time the therapist should endeavour to develop the stamina needed to absorb and contain the impact of the disabled client's physical and psychological concerns.

A client's file can provide important information, but no matter how objectively and carefully it is written it contains other people's judgments and opinions, which could influence the therapist's view. Because disabled people are often treated in a patronising, infantilising manner it is important for the therapist to try to redress this imbalance by interacting directly and solely with the client. By doing so the therapist demonstrates trust in the client's capability. Another positive outcome is that the therapeutic space is left free from external influences and is thus available to work through the client's own perceptions.

LEARNING POINT

■ Even when therapists cannot understand a client's speech they should endeavour to resist the temptation to expose the relationship to a third party so as to maintain dignity and develop intimacy and trust.

Ménage à trois

There were three of us in the room – Di, the computer and I. The computer had a big sign attached to it, saying 'WHAT I WRITE IS PRIVATE, DO NOT READ THE SCREEN' The therapeutic dyad had turned into triad, the third party beins the computer. What was the role of the computer and how did it evolve and change?

The computer created a chain of dependencies. At the beginning of the relationship I had been dependent on the occupational therapist for technical support. The client had sensed my inadequacy and tried to offer a crutch in the form of pretyped material. This could be seen as an equalising act. My 'disability' had been exposed when I accepted the computer and the help of the occupational therapist, so the client had reversed roles by offering support.

We were five weeks into therapy before I could trust myself to set up the computer for Di's use without help. When I became less anxious about the computer I noticed that our seating arrangement actually resembled a triangle. The computer was on the table and Di and I sat side by side in front of it. Di was typed 'Last Friday, Paula, my key worker, went sick over the weekend; I was alone.' I replied, 'You are sorry for Paula's troubles and also for yourself, as you feel lonely without her. Perhaps you are also saying to me that you are feeling lonely here because I am paying attention to the computer, rather than to you.' Di responded with a big smile of relief and typed 'I like Paula very much she knows everything about me.' This response could be seen as a validation of the interpretation in the form of a displaced image of a well-functioning person, a reflection of a positive, unconscious, introjective identification.

A few weeks later Di typed. 'Next week I will have a week off.' This comment made me feel surprised and guilty at the same time. I said, 'By telling me that you will not be here next week, you are also reminding me that we have not agreed on letting each other know about breaks and missed sessions.' I was moved by Di's clear assertion. Shamefully, my surprise at Di's decision to take time off came from the fact that I had allowed her disability to limit my expectations and probably projected onto her a degree of dependency, which I believe was triggered by my own sense of helplessness and dependency on the occupational therapist's technical ability.

The effect of the break was twofold: it created a space and it slowed the pace. The break also tested how client and therapist would survive a separation and the anxiety it might trigger. In the session after the break, for the first time Di typed messages about her family: how she was missing her dead mother and father, and how concerned she was about her sister, who was working too hard. Di had needed a break before she could feel safe enough to trust me with her own world.

At the end of each session Di saved the text, and at the beginning of the next she brought back to the screen the last message from the previous session. Then one day I could not find the computer and Di indicated that it had been left on the ambulance. This was a challenge, not to have a third party. I realised that I had become accustomed to, and perhaps also dependent on, the presence of a 'chaperone' to keep an eye on us. We kept to the usual seating arrangement, sitting side by side in front of the table but looking at each other instead of the screen. I said, 'Perhaps the computer was left because you are a bit fed up with it. Although the computer helps us to be precise and accurate, it is also coming between us.' At the time I did not admit that I too was a bit fed up with the computer and the lengthy and tedious typing process. I believe that Di unconsciously knew that I was talking about myself as well. That session, despite Di having to repeat each word several times before I could understand it, we did communicate directly, although some words were probably lost or misunderstood. Di talked about her mother and sister. She said that she was still worried about her sister working too hard, and that she loved her. Di's worry about her sister may also have reflected her concern about the therapist working too hard. A few weeks later Di went on a five-week holiday. Was this long break an unconscious attempt on the client's part to look after the therapist, to give her a break so that she would not become sick and die as her parents had?

When Di arrived at the first session after the break she was again without the computer – this time it had been left at home. She said, 'I am happy, I am in love, he lives not far away. I met him at Lourdes, he is somebody I knew before.' She went on to talk about visiting her mother's grave with her sister and brother. Then she said, 'I want to go to Lourdes and to be a leader. I know how, some of the leaders are not very good. I could be a better one. But I don't know how to do it. I want you to tell my key worker about it.' I was somewhat surprised by Di's perception of herself as more able than a non-disabled person. It is possible that the emotional state of being in love had linked to early experiences of being loved by her mother to strengthen Di's ego and motivate her to put her ability to the test. Despite being severely disabled, Di perceived herself as able and loveable. Lussier (1980, p. 184), in his fascinating paper 'The Physical Handicap and the Body Ego', maintains that 'for the physically normal person, the fantasmic threat of a handicap, castration or disintegration, through objective identification, could have more neurotic impact than a real congenital handicap for the handicapped person him or herself. The psychic reality has more power than the objective reality.' Di's positive view of herself supports Lussier's argument that disability can only ever be a relational concept. The way she perceived and presented herself indicated that (probably due to a strong maternal bond) her internal good object had stayed intact and was unscathed by her profound disability.

Or was it an omnipotence fantasy? Did her wish to become a leader reflect an inability to distinguish between reality and fantasy? Perhaps her lack of rivalrous competition with peers had led to unrealistic aspirations. How could she know her limitations if she had never measured herself against others?

But were her aspirations unrealistic, or did questioning her ability indicate a form of prejudice? Di was entirely dependent on others for survival and daily care, and her ability to communicate was limited because it was difficult for others to understand her words.

For a moment I was unable to share Di's belief in herself and her hopes for the future. In an almost ritualistic way she kept repeating 'I want to become a leader but I don't know how to go about it.' She was also telling me that the way I led the therapeutic encounter was not good enough. She would be a better leader but she was not yet sure how to do it; neither was I.

It may seem paradoxical that Di waited patiently for me to master the computer and then abandoned it. Let us look at this process from a developmental perspective. The computer had been invested with the role of transitional object (Winnicott, 1958); that is, the computer represented mother and therapist in their absence, thus fulfilling the adaptive function of working through the absolute loss of the dead mother and the temporary loss of the therapist between sessions and during breaks. Like a child who uses a doll to replace her mother until dependency turns into self-reliance, Di was using the computer until she felt safe enough to trust herself in the new relationship.

Before we can let go of a person, a habit or an object we first have to get to know who they are and how they affect our life. As the old saying goes, 'You can't let go of something you've never had'. So getting to know the computer was a necessary stage in the process of letting it go. Convinced that the computer, the third party, was an obstacle, I believed that until I could operate it independently I would be under its spell. Unconsciously Di knew that I needed to master the computer before we could to let go of it. The computer had been left on the ambulance and at home only when Di was sure that I was able to set it up and use it entirely on my own.

Letting go of the transitional object

Slowly the role of the computer in our relationship had changed and Di no longer needed to 'forget' to bring it. In the early stages of therapy I would prepare the computer for use and as soon as Di came in she would hold out her hand for me to put on the wrist-switch. Now she ignored the computer and approached me directly, using her limited vocal sounds. Another aspect of the letting go process concerned the saving of the text. In the past Di had been careful to save the text after each session, but she stopped doing it now, trusting that we could pass words between us without the help of the machine. The computer lost its high status as life-support machine when we discovered that we could communicate through Di's slurred speech and my interpretations, however imperfect. From that point onwards Di would put her hand out for the computer switch only when we got stuck because I was unable to decipher her words. Then I would fit the switch to her wrist and she would type the word I had not understood. As soon as the obstacle had been overcome Di would return to speech.

The computer had become an occasional tool to be used or not used as Di saw fit. It no longer dominated the relationship, and I no longer felt anxious about it. It had returned to its original job as Di's ally. Nevertheless Di still resorted to typing when her statements were less believable. For example in a session where she talked about her loneliness and how unfair it was that her boyfriend was unavailable to her, she typed 'Good news – I am going to be a leader, my sister is going to have a baby.' In the next session she talked again about her boyfriend not turning up, and then typed 'He really wants to go out with me.' I said, 'Perhaps by typing and seeing the words on the screen it becomes easier to believe in what you are saying.' Di said 'Yes, I feel lonely, every day I want to be happy, I don't know how to tell him. I miss my mum.' I replied, 'Perhaps the fact that I don't always understand you makes you feel lonely and frustrated, longing for someone who would understand you like your mum did.' She responded, 'My sister loves me and Paula knows me, she can help me, I don't want to be lonely every day I want to be happy.'

Di's talk about positive figures such as her sister who loved her and Paula who knew her can be seen as validation of my interpretation that Di's frustration was the result of her communication difficulties. But she still felt lonely. Although I took responsibility for my shortcomings I could not rectify the situation. I could not make our communication any better. All that I could offer was to stay with the frustration.

The Four Phases of the Therapeutic Relationship

The initial phase of the therapeutic relationship have some similarity to the symbiotic period of the human infant in the mother–child dyad. According to Mahler (1968), symbiosis precedes separation/individuation. Greenberg and Mitchell (1983, p. 281) suggest that 'during the symbiotic period libidinal cathexis is directed toward a "dual-unity" that includes the object (mother) as well as the self. At the same time it cannot be an object relationship, because there is no, or very little, differentiation between the self and the object.' The term symbiosis was first used by De Bary (1987), a nineteenth-century biologist, to describe how certain species depend on one another for their survival, for example a particular species of bird pecks food off the teeth of the rhinoceros, to the benefit of both. The mother–child dyad only approximates symbiosis because the infant may depend on the mother for survival but the mother's physical survival does not depend on the infant. It seems that in my therapeutic relationship with Di the roles of mother and infant alternated among the three parties involved in the relationship: the client, the therapist and the computer. The way in which the therapeutic process evolved can be divided into four phases that parallel the stages of human development.

Phase one: the referral procedure and pretherapy interactions

From the first step taken by the client to obtain therapy the ground rules and framework of therapy become an active and critical force (Langs, 1997). The referral procedure for Di, which preceded the first session, consisted of four steps and involved at least four people:

■ Step 1: the client sought therapy – Di asked her centre key worker to arrange counselling.
■ Step 2: the client's representative made a referral – on Di's behalf the key worker made a referral to the psychotherapist, and told the occupational therapist about the referral.

- Step 3: third-party intervention – the occupational therapist talked to the psychotherapist about Di's communication problems and the computer was presented as the solution.
- Step 4: the therapist allowed impingement – the therapist agreed to include the computer in Di's therapy and to liaise with the occupational therapist for technical help.

As we can see, confidentiality and privacy between therapist and client was compromised by the involvement of the key worker and the occupational therapist. The therapist's neutrality was impaired by accepting the occupational therapist's advice about the computer prior to meeting with the client, revealing to the client her insecurity and anxiety. By allowing all those factors to impinge at the start of the therapeutic relationship a pattern of deviation was put in place that would later affect the therapist's ability to secure the therapeutic frame.

The environment in which I saw Di was that of an institution, which like most institutions was invested by staff and users with the task of providing safety and a sense of belonging. In reality most institutions are not designed to fulfil this purpose (Menzies-Lyth, 1988). Two assumptions about care-providing institutions are that clients could not survive on their own outside the institution and that workers are in constant need of advice and help. However all this care and support does not prevent death, pain and impairment, and the frustration that follows provokes anxiety and defences that prevent learning through trial and error. For people in institutions, error and uncertainty may symbolise the threat of destruction, which when dealing with pain and death seems intolerable. Therapists who work in an institutional context are caught in the vicious cycle of allowing impingement in the form of help and support, which in turn results in infringement of privacy, confidentiality and anonymity. In Di's case this was coupled with my anxiety about a relationship with a client who, so it seemed, could not speak. Lack of speech can evoke fantasies of regression to primitive levels of animal behaviour, and therapists may unconsciously experience fear of losing both the thin veneer of human civilisation that is held by speech and the protection against death anxiety that the use of language offers in the form of reasoning, planning and strategising. Such disturbing fantasies can lead to mishandling of the ground rules and result in frame deviation.

The forthcoming relationship with Di felt like embarking on an adventure. A person who had been described as unable to speak had requested therapy, but how was it going to work? I experienced excitement, curiosity and anxiety all at the same time. Therefore when the occupational therapist offered what seemed like a first aid package, consisting of information about the client's communication problem and a computer, I was glad to displace the anxiety of the unknown and unpredictable and challenge my technophobia by accepting her advice and technical support. However in order to reduce my anxiety I had allowed an impingement on the as yet unformed relationship.

Phase two: building trust

Splitting as a defence against anxiety

The main characteristics of my first meeting with Di were avoidance and acting out. The presence of the computer on the table in front of us offered the opportunity to avoid eye contact. The anxiety that is normally experienced by client and therapist alike at the first meeting was intensified by the speech difficulty. The inadequacies became the unwanted bad objects. According to Klein (1946) the primitive first stage of development is the paranoid-schizoid position. The unwanted internal bad objects are projected onto an external element and the good objects are retained. In this first session both Di and I were trying to split the 'good' from the 'bad' by seeking an external element onto which to project our bad objects. For the technophobic therapist the computer qualified as an ideal candidate for projecting bad objects.

The computer acquired the role of an Orwellian 'Big Brother'. We did not relate to each other. Instead each of us related to the computer, which was given the power to control the relationship. This construct resembled that of two siblings who communicate only through the mother/computer, which in turn becomes a persecutory object through projective identification: 'When projection is mainly derived from the infant's impulse to harm or to control the mother, he feels her to be the persecutor' (Klein, 1946, quoted in Mitchell, 1986, p. 183). The computer became the 'bad mother', and thus shielded me from becoming the 'bad object'.

Managing the therapeutic frame

During this early phase, setting the ground rules was a challenge. Time-keeping was extremely difficult because it could take as long as 40 minutes for Di to type one sentence. I felt an urge to compensate, to extend the session time. I recognised a wish to modify the frame and had to remind myself, as Searles (1973, p. 258) puts it, that 'reliability, whether expressed in punctuality, regularity or sitting arrangements must have to do with both participants developing sureness as to what the situation will and will not permit'. Perhaps one of the most difficult aspects of being a therapist is becoming aware of internal and external pressures to change and modify the therapeutic frame, especially when an excuse is provided by working with a disabled client.

Phase three: towards autonomy, consolidation and letting go

The two occasions when Di 'forgot' the computer could be viewed as the use of neutral or neutralised aggression in the service of the ego, which helps to accept separateness without being overwhelmed by anxieties such as fear of loss of love, separation and castration anxiety (Mahler *et al.*, 1975, p. 226). Forgetting the computer was an innocent act that neutralised my aggression towards the machine and created a new environment, albeit temporarily. Both Di and I entered a phase similar to the depressive position, 'in which the infant recognises a whole object and relates himself to this object (Segal, 1975, p. 68) We were ready to let go of the split facilitated by the computer and to experience each other as whole objects. We both summoned up the courage for the real adventure. Like Mahler *et al.*'s (1975) description of the little boy Teddy, who could walk but could not let go, we had to hold on to the computer. But gradually, like a toddler who takes a step or two and then goes back to the safety of the parent, Di began to take her solo steps in therapy. Perhaps one of the reasons for her slow pace was to ensure that I too was ready for the adventure. The client was looking after the therapist, as suggested by Searles' (1965) idea of 'the patient as a therapist to the analyst'. Proving that at times the client can mother the therapist introduced an equalising element into the therapeutic relationship. Paradoxically, 'supporting' the therapist opened the way for the client to engage with her own infant need to regress and project onto the therapist the role of nurturing mother.

Phase four: making choices and taking risks

We had survived the passive aggression expressed through the forgotten computer and the two breaks, and it was now time for reparation. Di was prepared to tolerate my difficulty with deciphering her speech and ready not be humiliated or frightened by our mutual stumbling. She accepted my 'disability' – my limited ability to understand her – and now believed that it was possible to work together despite our difficulties.

When the computer was put aside my disability became visible. The intimacy that was made possible by removing the third party allowed the mirroring aspect of the mother–infant relationship to enter into the therapeutic process. Greenacre (1958, p. 618) states that 'The sense of identity involves comparison and contrast with some emphasis on basic likenesses, but with special attention called to obvious unlikenesses.' The effort to translate the sounds that Di produced into familiar words and my occasional need to admit that I was unable to do so had a very sobering effect, but it promoted mutual respect and allowed the intimacy and relatedness to develop gradually. We had reached the stage that Searles' (1959) calls 'therapeutic symbiosis', which he sees as the phase preceding individuation. Di was determining the pace. During the last few sessions in the period reported here, Di was considering the possibility of reducing her days in the day centre from four to one a week so that she could continue with therapy and go back to college.

LEARNING POINT

■ A client who seeks 'talking therapy' but lacks the ability to communicate verbally can challenge the professional confidence of a therapist. How can a person without speech ask for psychotherapy, which hinges on the exchange of speech?

IMPLICATIONS FOR THERAPISTS

The four phases described above could be compared to the developmental stages, where the construct of the mother–child relationship is used as a framework for the therapeutic process.

■ Phase one: the referral is like the prenatal fantasy stage where the mother is told that there is a problem with the foetus. Her anxiety weakens her trust in her maternal ability and she allows others to take over some of her responsibilities.
■ Phase two: for the therapist, realising the degree of the client's limitations can be likened to a mother realising the limitations of her impaired baby. The therapist, like some primary caregivers, may then be tempted to create a barrier that will prevent her from relating directly to her different than expected baby/client. Seeking the intervention of other professionals is one way of creating a

distance. An extension such as Di's computer can offer a range of disengagement strategies: it can serve as a barrier, as a third party and perhaps as a father figure. In the last role it could be expected to support and protect the mother–baby or therapist–client dyad.

■ Phase three: a dyad slowly replaces the triad – the client/infant tries to let go of the dependency on the computer/third party. The process of letting go (forgetting the computer) includes an element of aggression, which may feel like an attack on the therapeutic relationship. A successful venture means that all three survive the attack, which leads to the development of intimacy, with client and therapist relating directly to each other.

■ Phase four: once the child/client and mother/therapist have faced and accepted each other and their own differences/disabilities, the third party is used only as and when client or therapist feel the need for support. Awareness of the implications of the third party will prevent impingements on the relationship. New discoveries and creativity become possible when the present reality has been integrated.

The constant effort to keep to the ground rules and secure the frame, although not always fully achieved, is pivotal to the survival and effectiveness of any complicated therapeutic relationship.

Summary

Di's story is of particular interest because of the way her paralysis and limited speech affected the therapeutic process. Her physical dependency at times masked her independent free spirit. The need to use an external object in the form of a computer to communicate hindered the development of intimacy, yet enabled Di to choose how to relate to others.

6

DISABILITY AND SEXUALITY

What Does Disability Do to Sex?

The sexual problems of the disabled are aggravated by a widespread view that they are either malignantly sexual, like libidinous dwarfs or, more commonly, completely asexual. (Murphy, 1987)

In previous chapters the narrative revolved around one main representative character to illustrate the therapeutic interaction with a disabled person in a specific stage of the human life cycle. Because sexuality is not a stage but an integral part of the human condition, this chapter will not follow the story of one individual. Instead several vignettes will be presented, each illustrating a specific aspect of how disability can affect the way in which sexuality is experienced or expressed. It is interesting to note that the subject of human sexuality has been given considerable coverage the psychotherapeutic literature but little if any attention has been paid to the effect of disability on human sexuality.

As with most minority groups there is discrepancy between the way in which group members perceive themselves and how they are perceived by the rest of society. The question to be investigated is: why is it that disabled people are frequently seen as either oversexed, as in perversion, or as lacking any sexual drive or interest? What can be the reason for perceiving disabled people as occupying only the extremes of the human sexuality scale, pushing them outside the main sexual playing field?

Love and Intimacy

Acquired disability

At about the time of his fortieth birthday Fred was diagnosed as having multiple sclerosis (MS). MS is difficult to diagnose and it took a long time for the doctors to arrive at their conclusion. At first Fred was told that his type of MS was non-progressive, which meant that apart from occasional discomfort he would be able to rely on his body functioning for many years to come. Unfortunately this prognosis was wrong and within four years he had deteriorated to such an extent that he was losing muscle control in various parts of his body and was hardly able to walk.

During his first session of therapy Fred talked about his medical condition, the confusing prognosis and his family's difficulty with accepting the fact that he was disabled. Then he stopped and fell into a silence, his face contorted with pain and discomfort. Long minutes passed before he blurted out, 'I need to digress, it is about sex, I am impotent, I can't have sex.' He paused, tensed and waited for a response.

This was a tender moment, and the therapist's reaction at that point would go a long way towards shaping the nature of the therapeutic relationship. The therapist tried to organise her thoughts. The statement 'I am impotent, I can't have sex' had followed a detailed description of Fred's perception of the unreliable and disappointing systems that were suppose to support him. Fred felt that he had been let down by his body, the medical profession and his own family. While the therapist had been listening to Fred's narrative she had thought to herself. 'This man's existence is strewn with complicated survival problems, fears of the future and ongoing frustrations. Yet he talks about his inability to perform sexually as the main cause of his distress. What could this be about? Perhaps Fred is unconsciously concerned about my motive for seeing him, and is testing my capacity to accept an impotent man?' The therapist, still somewhat puzzled, just said 'Perhaps you want to say a bit more about it.' In her intervention she was trying to address Fred's discomfort when he raised the sexual issue; she wanted to estab-lish that there were no taboo subjects. She was also hoping to ascertain whether the word 'impotent' was being applied to his disability, his sexuality or both.

Fred responded, 'My wife does not let me touch her; she turns her back to me whenever I try to get near her. Her father thinks I am making it all up. I am a very good accountant but I have lost my busi-ness.' Fred was not just talking about his inability to perform sexually, he was also talking about his inability to perform as the man he wanted to be. He was talking about his losses, about the lack of intimacy between him and his wife and his father in-law's lack of trust in him. In this short comment, past, present, disability, relationships and sexual identity were interwoven into the broad canvas of his life.

When faced with such complexity a therapist might be tempted to simplify matters by focusing mainly on the link between the client's sexual incapacity and the physical effects of MS. Such an approach would allow clear and simple reasoning. However, this would be a narrow and reductionist approach. Any therapist who listened carefully to Fred's response would recognise that other forces, some preceding the onset of disability, were affecting and shaping his perceived experiences.

Becoming disabled in mid-life meant that Fred had to struggle with unexpected losses, such as the deterioration of bodily functions, the erosion of his status as breadwinner, and his shattered hopes for the future. His main concern was his ability to remain active as a man, husband and father. It became clear during therapy that other losses and disappointments had been projected into his current sexual and relationship difficulties.

Fred's mid-life experience of disability brought with it the loss of love and intimacy. What if any, is, the sexual significance of the time in life at which a person becomes disabled? In order to address this question we shall consider the experience of a person who was impaired from birth.

LEARNING POINTS

■ Although MS can affect sexual performance, the physical aspect is just one of many factors that add to the complexity of the person's life.
■ Fred's predicament demonstrated how the onset of disability can bring to the surface painful and unresolved difficulties.

Congenital disability

Dan, who was 23 years old, told his therapist that although the girl he loved said she loved him too, she was relating to him in a sisterly manner, avoiding any possibility of sexual intimacy. It was confusing and did not make sense. Before seeking psychotherapeutic help Dan had told his GP about his problem and had been referred to the local hospital for sex therapy. This experience left him both disappointed and humiliated. He said furiously, 'What do they think I am, a machine? It is not what to do that I need to learn, it is why it does not work for me, why Laura does not fancy me.' The 'me' in Dan's comment needed attention – he did not need a sex manual, he needed an understanding of his unique predicament.

Despite the fact that his legs and one arm had been deformed and partially paralysed since birth, Dan had gone to mainstream schools and lived at home. He had just been awarded with a degree in business studies and was looking for work. He had not been institutionalised. He was familiar with the non-disabled world, well-informed and aware of his sexuality. He was able to form close emotional relationships with women. Yet these had always remained platonic, leaving him sexually frustrated and confused. He could not understand what was blocking the development of sexual intimacy, why the woman he loved was treating him like an asexual being. Why did she tell him all about her relationships with other men, didn't she recognise the pain she was causing?

Several months into therapy Dan became aware that he was angry with his body – he despised the look of this body, which he felt had let him down. This realisation allowed him to understand that as long as he treated his body with contempt, others, including his girlfriend, would tend to avoid contact with it. At about that time his orthopedic consultant suggested a risky and complicated experimental surgical procedure that offered some hope of improving his stature. After deliberating at length Dan decided to go ahead with it.

What led him to such a decision? Perhaps one of the main determents was that he did not feel like a whole person – he felt like a eunuch. He had internalised the message that his body was not loveable as it was. As a newborn baby his mother had been unable to show him the full acceptance and love that he had needed to develop a positive self-image. Dan's need for 'mirroring' (Kohut, 1978; Winnicott, 1971) had not been met. He had never been made to feel perfect and loved, but different, imperfect and difficult to love because of the way he was. It seemed that his decision to have the operation was in part an expression of self-hatred or mutilation or castration by proxy. It could be interpreted as 'This is a bad body, no one wants this body as it is. My mother never liked it, my girlfriend does not like it, I hate it, and therefore it has to go under the knife.' Although this seemed aggressive or even violent, it was invested with the hope, however slim, that a new, reformed and loveable body would emerge from the pain and suffering.

What are the differences and similarities between Fred and Dan? Both of them had experienced the loss of the wished-for-body, the object of love and desire, regardless of their age and the stage in the life when they became disabled. They perceived their 'body in the world' as poorly functioning and unlovable. Underlying this was the familiar tension between the desire for a perfect body and the inevitable imperfection of the human body. Although this is a universal conflict, the presence of impairment can exacerbate it by pointing out the gap not only between the body as it is and the wished-for body but also between disabled and non-disabled bodies. Those whose body lays furthest from the wished-for body may find themselves marginalised or even excluded. The attempts by non-disabled individuals to eliminate their perceived imperfections may impair the disabled person's already fragile sense of belonging and further inhibit the possibility of intimacy.

Physical and mental impairment or ugliness has been used since time immemorial to signify badness, evil or moral deviance, thus effectively casting impaired individuals out of the community. In his study of English cultural history, Keith Thomas (1971) found that as late as the eighteenth century, doctors and midwifes in England believed that deformed children might well result from indecent sexual acts and that the morally deviant state of mind of the coupling parties helped to give the embryo its distinctive shape. Valerie Sinason (1992) provides an interesting analysis of Shakespeare's portrayal of the thoughts of Richard III:

> But I, that am not shap'd for sportive tricks,
> Nor made to court an amorous looking-glass;
> I – that am rudely stamp'd, and want love's majesty
> To strut before a wanton ambling nymph;
> I – that am curtail'd of this fair proportion;
> Cheated of feature by dissembling nature,
> Deform'd, unfinish'd, sent before my time
> Into this breathing world, scarce half made up . . .
> (*Richard III*, I, i, 14–21)

Thus Richard III reveals how bearers of impairment feel 'rudely stamped' by the sexual act that created them. Unlike non-disabled children, who try to deny that their existence is due to their parents' lovemaking, children born with an impairment feel connected to that sexual act. Their hatred of parental sexuality is often displaced onto themselves or others. Society's negative and often denigrating reaction to disability contributes to their perception that they must be the result of bad intercourse.

LEARNING POINT

■ For people who have been disabled since birth, sexual concerns include not just their own physical and relational experiences but also the sexual act that brought them into the world, which some perceive as the cause of their impairment.

Sexuality and the Developmental Process

In this section we shall look at some traditional ideas on the developmental process and examine how impairment can affect the development of an infant or child. According to Freud's libido theory there are a number of psychosexual stages, which are determined by the age at which the oral, the anal, the phallic and then the genital region dominate the infant's inner life. Each of these stages affects the infant's reactions, needs and ability to symbolise. Normality, according to Freud, is the outcome of passing through each stage in sequence, so should we assume that if one misses out a stage or fails to move on, one is heading towards fixation and perversion?

This concept of normality seems rigid and narrow. It certainly does not leave much room for the infant whose body does not allow full participation in each stage. In his *Three Essays on Sexuality* (Freud, 1905, p. 160) Freud says:

> No healthy person, it appears, can fail to make some addition that might be called perverse to the normal sexual aim; and the universality of this finding is in itself enough to show how inappropriate it is to use the word perversion as a term of reproach. In the sphere of sexual life we are brought up against peculiar, and, indeed, insoluble difficulties as soon as we try to draw a sharp line to distinguish mere variation within the range of what is physiological from pathological symptoms.

The ambiguity that is being expressed here about sexuality seems to reflect the tension between the tendency to classify as a means of clarifying and predicting, and the unpredictable and complex reality. The wish to distinguish between what is normal and therefore acceptable and what is not normal and therefore perverse plays an important part in the way we relate both to disability and sexuality.

In Lussier's (1980) view, disability is in the eye of the beholder. Peter, who was born with deformed and very short arms, did not see himself as incapacitated in any way. The problem he struggled with was the need to prove to others, mainly his parents, that although he was not perfect he was normal like all other children, or even better.

The concepts of narcissism and body image are tied together in the development of self-identity as the composite of psychological self and body self. A person with a congenital disability knows no other body, and his or her developing ego, identity and body image are subject to the same parenting needs as any other child. Greenacre (1958) puts forward the idea that self-image which is, intimately related to body image, is the basis on which one's sense of identity is built. She writes, 'The individual is in need of at least one other person, similar to himself, to look at and to speak to in order to feel safe in his own identity' (Ibid, p. 625). Greenacre consider, that the face and the genitals are the most important body parts in this process.

Lussier (1980, p. 183) takes Greenacre's idea a step further and suggests that 'The mother as well as the child needs a similar person, a similar body in order to be led to achieve the necessary fusion with the child.' According to Lussier the mother's unconscious interpretation of dissimilarity can be seen as a castration threat, or as a threat of ego disintegration through the loss of a body part. The anxiety caused by physical dissimilarity can cause the mother to withdraw psychologically from her baby in order to protect herself from loss of identity.

In addition to her unconscious concern about her own ego integrity, comes the near conscious narcissistic blow of not producing a perfect child. The child will not reflect for the mother and the mother will not reflect for the child. The primary identification will be impaired. In order to be able to reach her disabled child the mother needs an amazing degree of ego integrity, emotional security and harmony with her own body self. The child will relate to his body in the same way as his mother relates to it. Lussier concludes that the problem is not the actual physical difference, but the ability of the parents to adapt and to deal with their own emotions, such as guilt, shame and pity.

When Freud (1905) developed his sequence of psychosexual phases he believed these to be based on an intrinsic developmental process driven by biological forces and on a predetermined maturation of needs. Freud is quite adamant that physical sexual characteristics do not parallel mental characteristics or sexual attitudes and behaviour.

Al was paralysed from birth. He had very limited movement and could not speak. His limitations prevented him from experiencing and expressing the physical manifestations of the psychosexual stages as he was unable to control or manipulate most parts of his body. At the age of 21 he received a computerised voice synthesiser and for the first time in his life he was able to express himself in words. For the first two weeks the computer emitted an avalanche of 'dirty talk', Al's vocabulary consisting mainly of words with sexual connotations. The members of staff at his institution were horrified and thought that the word synthesiser had unleashed a monster. They found it hard to understand how this helpless and quiet person, who had never uttered a word before, was now producing a barrage of verbal abuse. It took some time for them to appreciate that he was trying to catch up on his developmental process, that he was using his newly acquired means of expression and communication to demonstrate his sexual interest and to learn what effect this had on others. Although his body was deformed and paralysed, his mind was full of sex. Despite institutionalisation a sexually repressive environment and the fact that his physical restrictions had prevented him from progressing through all the psychosexual phases, he appeared to have a lively interest in sexual matters.

The libido – the sexual urges that provide the motivation for psychic functioning – of disabled young people does not seem to be significantly different from that of non-disabled young people. However their physical restrictions may limit and sometimes prevent progress through the psychosexual stages of the developmental process (oral, anal, phallic and genital), as traditionally understood. How can the oral stage be completed when the satisfaction gained from sucking is not possible due to rigid facial muscles? How can the body be discovered and experienced when children do not have control over their own hands and cannot touch themselves or others? Can it still be said that the only way to reach sexual maturity is to possess a fully formed and functioning body? These questions remain open because the research conducted so far is insufficient in that it is based mainly on individual case studies.

Anthony says, 'As a disabled person from birth, I never had the luxury of such attributes as dignity and pride, or being imbued with a sense of macho superiority' (Shakespeare *et al.*, 1996, p. 117). Anthony is painfully aware of being different. So is Christopher Nolan, who was paralysed from birth, has no speech and finds it difficult to swallow. He writes in his poetic autobiographical novel: 'He never sobbed upon his loss, but cemetery dampness clung in the air as he watched boys pairing off with girls and girls while masking yes beamed no, meaning giggle some maybe' (Nolan, 1988, p. 179). Nolan, although unable to participate, is fully aware of sexual courting behaviour. He sees himself as 'a celibate pilgrim through life'.

LEARNING POINTS

- The mystery that still surrounds the human developmental process and the complexity of social and parental attitudes are the main factors affecting the sexuality of disabled people.
- For those disabled from birth. The opportunity to engage in perusing and expressing sexual interest is limited by physical capability and social attitudes.

IMPLICATION FOR THERAPISTS

■ Before addressing the client's sexual physical and emotional differences, therapists must deal with their own unresolved issues regarding
sexuality and body self.

Sex and Guilt

In Western Judeo-Christian culture, sex is wrapped up with guilt and
punishment. The Biblical punishment for what Christians call the original sin was: 'I will greatly multiply thy sorrow and thy conception; in
sorrow thou shalt bring forth children; and thy desire shall be to thy
husband and he shall rule over thee' (*Genesis* 4–16). Sexual desire and
the regeneration process have since been closely linked to if not identified with guilt and punishment.

Helen, who contracted crippling rheumatoid arthritis at the age of
42, said 'I don't want ever to have sex again. God has punished me by
making my body painful and repulsive.' For Helen, sex, guilt and punishment were synonymous. Reality and fantasy were mixed together in
her attempt to grapple with the pain and fear brought about by disability. In Western culture sex has other negative connotations. For
example if celibacy, as in the case of monks, nuns and Catholic priests,
is a way of moving nearer to God, then sexual activity must keep one
away from God. So in a time of crisis when the individual feels the
need to be protected by God as the all-powerful parental figure, becoming celibate, as Helen did, is a logical step.

Melanie Klein (1952) suggested that anxiety and guilt increase the
need to externalise bad figures and internalise good ones; to attach
desire, love, guilt and reparative tendencies to some objects, and hate
and anxiety to others. When disability is perceived as a punishment the
distinction between good and bad becomes blurred. Confusing thoughts
may trouble some disabled individuals, such as 'Will I be accepted now,
as I have already paid for my sins? (whatever they may be), or 'Is my
badness so great that it necessitates such a severe punishment?'

Disability and sexuality both have the power to invoke guilt and
fear, stemming from archaic psychical and cultural roots. Whenever
we feel guilty we defend ourselves against it by pushing it away from
our conscious mind – we try to avoid and deny the disturbing issue. As
one doctor reports: 'I have done many consultations about youngsters
with disability for private physicians, and I have never had one say:
"You know, the problem with this youngster and his family is that he

never asks anything about sex." It is not thought of as a problem to deal with' (quoted in Bullard and Knight, 1981, p. 82). This illustrates the all too familiar situation in which professionals, families and the disabled person collude in the effort to avoid or deny the possibility that the disabled person is also a sexual being.

In 1986 I had the task of organising an activity for disabled people at a day centre. Assuming that sex education might have been lacking for some of them I suggested watching a documentary film on the subject. The film was of four disabled people talking about their experience of finding out about sex. Maria, a young woman of 22 was in the audience. She had been educated away from home in a special school because of her cerebral palsy, which affected her mobility and speech. She was an outgoing, bright and articulate person. At one point the people in the film were discussing masturbation. Few minutes later Maria turned around and said, 'What is masturbation, what are they talking about?' I thought, 'How is it that a woman like Maria does not know what masturbation is; what is the reason for her ignorance? Could it be that her disability has impaired her sexuality to such an extent as to prevent natural curiosity and interest in sexual matters?' Yet this explanation did not fit with the fact that Maria had chosen to go and watch a film that had been advertised as dealing with sex education, and that she was interested and curious enough to ask what masturbation was.

Such ignorance is not a rare occurrence. Another example is Neal, who at the age of 29 told his therapist that until very recently he had not been aware that apart from the voice and external appearance there were other meaningful differences between the male and the female body. At the age of 29 Neal made a discovery that is usually made by the age of two.

Maria and Neal, like many disabled people, had not had the opportunity to discover their own body or that of others. This was due not only to their physical limitations but also to being closely watched by the adults who looked after them. Literally and metaphorically they lost touch with their body, and may have internalised a message that the body had to be kept hidden. In order to defend themselves against the pain of believing that the body they possess is undesirable or shameful, some people develop an equalising psychic construct that hides all body features from their awareness, male, female, disabled and non-disabled alike. It took Neal more than 20 years and a long spell of therapy to familiarise himself with his own body. Only when he no longer needed to hide his body could he begin to appreciate differences in the bodies of others. So perhaps such states of ignorance are caused by a combination of individual readiness and ability to receive and internalise sexual data, and the social and environmental context in which the young person's sexuality is encouraged or discouraged.

In Maria's case, she had been born to an Italian Catholic family and later sent to a special needs school. In different ways, both family and school had avoided addressing the question of sexuality. Nonetheless it was apparent that this young woman had developed, albeit later than her peer group, a healthy interest in sex and relationships. Both Neal and Maria had had restricted access to information and sexual exploration with other young people, not only due to their disability but also because their families and schools had perceived them as asexual, thus denying them sex information and education.

IMPLICATIONS FOR THERAPISTS

Should therapists act as the providers of missing sex education? The argument in favour of this additional role is that some clients are isolated and unable to gain access to information on the subject. It could be quite tempting for a therapist to become the bearer of vital information and by doing so become the 'good object', well separated from what could be perceived as the badness attached to such social and educational shortcomings. During internal debates and supervision discussions, therapists need to be reminded that their primary task is to help their clients to become aware of what is lacking so that when ready they will be able to engage in seeking and finding the missing aspects of their sexual knowledge and or experience. Although it is not part of therapists role to provide such information, in some circumstances it may be appropriate to alert other professionals to the gaps that have been revealed.

Gender Identity

Congenital disability

The question 'Who am I?' has been an integral part of the human quest for self-knowledge and indicates the ambiguity surrounding the notion of identity. Being a person with a disability adds to the problem of arriving at a consolidated identity. Developing a sense of individual identity, like any other choice, involves a loss, in this case the loss of fusion. McDougall (1989) describes the individuation process as repression of the contradictory wish to be an individual while remaining an indissoluble part of the 'other'. This wish is subsequently compensated by the acquisition of an unwavering sense of individual identity. In relation to sexual identity, McDougall asks what it is that allows the conviction that one's genitals are a unique possession and do not belong, for example, to one's parents. For non-disabled infants, perceiving themselves as similar to the parent of the same sex may bring a degree of certainty and reduce some of their anxiety. However most disabled infants would find it difficult to compare themselves to a parental figure because of their physical differences.

Striving for individuation and developing a sexual identity are essential components of the journey towards maturity. Being or becoming disabled adds even more obstacles to this difficult journey. Freud (1925) contributed to female oppression by portraying females not as unique, different beings, but as castrated males. Most adult females, however, have a role in society, despite their perceived inferiority. Blackwell-Stratten *et al.* (1988) argue that unlike non-disabled women, who have a societally sanctioned position as wife and mother, disabled women have no adult roles – not mother, not wife, not worker. Thus disabled women are perceived as having lost not only some of their ability, but also a great deal if not all of their womanhood. An anecdote quoted in Shakespeare *et al.* (1996, p. 66) illustrates this point:

> This head waiter that I knew well, I could speak Italian and we got on reasonably well, and he came up to me and said: 'You can't, can you . . .?' I said, 'Can't what?' . . . I knew what he meant, I thought, I'll drag this out a bit, and he said: 'Well, you can't have sex, can you?' and I said 'Why ever not?' and he said, 'Well, you can't walk . . .', and I said, 'You walk while you are having sex? I haven't seen that in the Kama Sutra!'

A Freudian interpretation of this would be that the legs are often seen as a phallic symbol. This unconscious fantasy may have led the waiter to his erroneous conclusion; the phallus represents sexuality, legs symbolise the phallus, therefore disfunctioning legs mean disfunctioning sexuality.

The positive and humorous response of the woman in this anecdote could well be linked to her being a woman and not a man. Being viewed as a castrated male, a woman starts at a lower rank than a man, so she is more accustomed to being seen as less able to function than male members of society and has developed ways of dealing with patronising and misinformed individuals.

If we accept Freud's idea that a male body is perfect, then any change is a loss rather then a gain. Gerschick and Miller (1995) investigated the clash between hegemonic masculinity and society's perception of disability as weakness. They interviewed 10 disabled men and identified three adaptive strategies:

■ Reformation, which entailed men redefining their masculinity according to their own terms.
■ Reliance, which entailed men internalising the traditional meanings of masculinity and attempting to meet them.
■ Rejection, which was about creating alternative masculine identities and subcultures.

The better adjusted were those who had rejected the social concept of masculinity, which they saw as problematic. In doing so they had created alternative gender practices. These were often linked to membership of the disability rights movement. One way of interpreting the finding of this study is that in order to reject the socially accepted masculine identity, another identity had to be found. This took form of 'coming out' as a disabled person. By adopting the disability movement as a social milieu or even an alternative family, the disabled person was able to create 'that which resembles me'. As Lichtenstein (1961) points out, subjective identity is always determined by two dimensions: 'that which resembles me' and 'that which is different from me'. Most disabled children grow up in an environment that offers them no resemblances and thus provides no role model. It is rare for a disabled child to be brought up by or be in close contact with a person who is similarly disabled. However in subsequent years it may become possible to identify with other disabled people. Once the identity of disabled people has been established as positive or even desirable, the mode of sexuality can be adjusted to their own physical reality, without the need to look up to or be compared with the non-disabled, mainstream sexual identity.

Acquired disability

The concept of change is central to the understanding of both the processes affecting the disabled person and the attitudes of non-disabled people. People with an acquired disability once lived in the mainstream of society. Their psychosexual development, body image and sexual experience were part of the varied and colourful tapestry that makes up the human experience. The reaction of each person who subsequently becomes disabled is different and unique. However some common experiences are shared by most newly disabled people, the most significant of which is losing the body that one has grown to know and to identify with, and acquiring a body that is different and new.

For most people, becoming disabled is a traumatic event whose magnitude the psyche is unable to process. People's reactions range from giving in to helplessness and impotency and regressing to the mother–baby state of dependency, to denying the emotional or even the physical effects of the event and pretending that nothing has really changed.

With regard to sex, one could argue that people with an acquired disability have enough obstacles to overcome in their everyday life and their libidinal energy would be better channelled into the struggle to survive in a difficult and often excluding environment. Sexuality is not uppermost on their mind. Indeed some disabled people may be completely unconcerned about sexual matters, in the same way as some non-disabled people opt for celibacy. But not all of them: 'To be totally honest, sex is one thing that torments my mind more than any other aspect of paralysis. In fact, for me, it has taken over my life as a constant obsession. A person without sexual feeling cannot be normal' (Spinal Injuries Association Newsletter, 1982, p. 16).

The physical aspects of sexual activity for people who acquire a disability in adult life require considerable maturity and the internal flexibility needed to adopt to a new way of being. Part of the problem lies in people's tendency to compare their current ability to perform and derive sexual pleasure, with their ability prior to the onset of disability. Some people may well give up, but others learn to turn their own disability or their partner's into an advantage. Bob was paralysed in an accident; Bernie, his partner, is a non-disabled woman. According to Bernie, 'One of the advantages for me of Bob not being able to physically do some things is that he's gotten into the habit of asking for what he wants. It's great when he says, "I'd really like to make love" or "I'd like to hug you" because I know that's what he wants, and I can decide whether that's what I want or not.' As for Bob, 'One thing I do know is that I am a much better lover now than I ever was before. There are a lot of reasons for that, but one of the biggest is that I am more relaxed. I don't have a list of do's and don'ts, a timetable or a proper sequence of moves to follow, or the need to give my partner an orgasm every time we make love. Sex isn't just orgasm for me; it's pleasuring, playing, laughing and sharing' (Bullard and Knight, 1981, p. 65).

When therapists work with disabled people it is essential for them to familiarise themselves with testaments carrying a positive message so that they could hold out hope for their clients from a position of knowing that it is possible for disabled people to be happily sexually active.

To be or not to be disabled is not the question, as it is very rarely a matter of choice. Although some disabled people say they would not want to change their fate, amongst non-disabled people disability is more often than not described as a 'tragedy', 'disaster', 'misfortune' and other negative adjectives. Yet as the story of Bob and Bernie demonstrates, when disability is taken just as another fact of life there can be positive aspects even in the delicate matter of sexual relations. The experience of disability may bring the realisation that sexual activity need not involve genital sensation and does not depend on sexual gymnastics but on the couple's capacity to weave their changing personal needs into the complex net of the total relationship.

Summary

The topic of disability and sexuality is vast but mostly untrodden. This chapter has not attempted to cover the whole subject. For example important issues such as sexual orientation amongst disabled people and the effect of the AIDS epidemic on disability and sexuality have not been touched upon. Instead the discussion has concentrated on the effect of physical difference on individuals' felt and perceived sexuality in order to offer the reader the awareness and understanding required to deal with the interface between sexuality and disability.

The reactions of others to one's disability can at times be more painful than the experience of disability itself. The perception of disabled people as asexual can cause suffering and confusion, as the following reveals: 'I walked around with an agonising crush on one boy for two years. The sexual feeling I had, I saw others having also, but they were not disabled. I thought: "I have these feelings, too, but I am ashamed because I realise I am not supposed to have them." So I walked around with a lot of emotional pain' (quoted in Bullard and Knight, 1981, p. 28). There are many more stories to illustrate the conflict between the way people with disability experience their sexuality and the overt or covert messages they constantly receive from society. Hugh, who was paralysed by a brain tumour, said to me: 'I once had a wife who was my lover, now I have a wife who is my nurse, but where is my lover? I know I have lost her, and I miss her so much, but I cannot tell her'.

Having a private space where intimate issues such as sex and love can be talked about and receive serious attention is a small step towards redressing the balance and enabling disabled people to hold on to their hopes and desires as whole and sexual human beings.

7

THE FINAL SEPARATION

Empedocles, the Greek philosopher, believed that one of the main principals of existence is the tension between love and strife (hate). When love rules all the elements are drawn together into a solid substance with no movement or distinction. When hate or strife rule all the elements separate into the smallest atoms and fly away from each other like dust. Neither of these options is conducive to life. According to Empedocles life depends on maintaining the tension between love and hate, between unification and separation. 'Birth is when we are snatched by strife and borne into this world of plurality' (Kirk and Raven, 1957, pp. 356–7).

Birth, Death and Separation

Human existence is on a continuum of separation that starts with separation from the womb at birth and ends with separation from life at death. Separation anxiety, which develops out of the infant's fear that its nurturing source will abandoned it, is a sign of becoming aware of the external world. This potentially paralysing fear is counterbalanced by what might be called the life force, the impulse to explore the external world creatively, which is the positive outcome of being loved and nurtured. The need for secure love and nurturing and the fear of loss and rejection are part of the human condition. For disabled people the consequences of losing the nurturing source differ from those of non-disabled people due to the complications and humiliations that are part and parcel of their everyday struggle. For example, imagine how it would feel to have to ask another person for help whenever you need to go to the toilet. Such potentially humiliating and frustrating experiences may toughen up the individual and bring out the will to defy and overcome adversity. But it also may encourage regression and overdependency. Whichever way we look at it, for disabled people the struggle to survive is usually much harder than it is for non-disabled people. Therefore the peace and rest attached to death may at times seem seductive and tempting.

Robert Murphy was in his late forties and at the height of his career as a professor of anthropology when he became paralysed as a result of a tumour in his spinal cord. In his autobiographical book *The Body Silent* he asks 'Is death preferable to disablement?' His answer is 'No, it is not, . . . life is at once its own means and its end, a gift that should neither be refused nor cast off, except in utmost extremity' (Murphy, 1990, p. 230). Publicly questioning the value of life as a disabled person and considering the option of giving up life were Murphy's way of externalising the inner conflict that psychoanalysts call the 'death wish' or 'death instinct'.

Freud (1920) identified a primary urge for self-destruction that he called the death instinct, as opposed to the life instinct of sexuality and self-preservation. In order to preserve ourselves we unconsciously direct the death instinct outwards, where it becomes the urge to harm and destroy others and is known as the aggression drive. According to Freud's pleasure principal, our psyche's main aim is to avoid pain or 'unpleasure'. Freud attributed pain and unpleasure to an increase in instinctual tension. He suggested that this tension could be released not only by action but also by dreaming or hallucinating about the satisfaction necessary for reducing the tension. The reality principal is juxtaposed against the pleasure principal, with its psychological capacity to come to grips with the external world. Sandor Ferenczi, the Hungarian contemporary of Freud, also believed that we are born with the wish to avoid the physical and psychical pain caused by the tension between the external experience of reality and the fantasy of unrestricted satisfaction. He suggested that the baby gives us the impression that 'he is far from pleased at the rude disturbance of the wish-less tranquillity he had enjoyed in the womb, and indeed that *he longs to regain this situation*' (Ferenczi, 1999, p. 71). We all, disabled and non-disabled alike, need to have a safe internal space that resembles the womb, in which we can imagine or recall being held and cared for by a good object.

When Ian was injured in a serious train collision he was in his mid thirties, was socially and professionally confident, and enjoyed a successful career, happy marriage and busy social life. His severe brain injury rendered him unable to walk or use his hands. He became quite irritated when people praised his courage: 'What do they mean when they say I am courageous? What other option do I have? If I don't push myself to stay alive I will die and I am not ready to die yet.' He was determined to retrieve some of the richness and pleasures that he knew life could offer. His 'life force' and early experience of secure love and nurturing and his adult experience as an autonomous individual were sustaining him in his uphill struggle. For Ian, life was a gift that he believed he deserved. Ron, however had different view of life.

The Story of Ron

Phase one: pretherapy interaction and the referral process

Ron was 44 years old when he asked to return to the day centre for disabled people. I had recently been appointed to the position of manager and did not know Ron, who had attended the centre before my time. Those members of staff who knew him did not welcome the idea of working with him again. I looked at his file to gain some understanding of the staff's reaction. As well as notes on his exclusion on the ground of aggressive and dangerous behaviour towards staff and other users of the centre there was considerable information on his history. At the age of three he had suffered convulsions that were followed by a coma lasting three weeks, resulting in spasticity to his left side. When he was 10, 'Aggressive behaviour and uncontrolled fits were treated by partial frontal Lobectomy and right Hemispherectomy' (GP's notes). When he was 13 his left arm was amputated. (Later on when, I became his therapist, Ron told me that he agreed to the amputation because people made fun of his claw-like left hand.) He was in his twenties when his father died, and he lived with his mother until she died when he was 40 years old. He was then admitted to a psychiatric unit but after three months was discharged into a local authority residential home. He was still living there when I first met him.

Ron came with his key worker to discuss the possibility of returning to the centre, and at the end of the meeting we agreed that he could attend regularly. During the discussion it had become clear that his aggressive behaviour was his way of expressing fear. I believe that it is the duty of institutions such as day centres, hospitals and schools to help contain the anxiety of disabled people, even when it is expressed in an aggressive manner.

While I was the manager of the centre, Ron often said to me, 'I know what you are doing, I'll burn this place and I will call the police to tell about you.' There were several times when Ron became aggressive towards women at the centre. He seemed to be in an emotional turmoil. Unfortunately the centre was only geared to dealing with the physical needs of its users and was not yet ready to offer psychotherapeutic help. We managed to arrange for him some brief counselling by the community mental health team.

Compromising neutrality

Shortly after Ron's counselling came to an end, I left my post at the day centre and moved on to develop a counselling service for people affected by disability. The centre was amongst the organisations that referred their users to the counselling service and Ron's key worker made a referral to the service on Ron's behalf. In the initial assessment session I checked with Ron, as I do with all indirect referrals, whether he had initiated the request for counselling or whether it had come from his key worker. Ron's firm reply was that he had asked for me to be his counsellor.

In an ideal world we would have waited for a counsellor who had had no previous relationship with Ron. However in the real world it was very unlikely that Ron would have another chance to receive counselling. This is because he was not only disabled but also institutionalised. There is considerable resistance amongst professionals to address the emotional experiences and internal life of disabled people when disability is combined with institutionalisation. Perhaps one of the reasons for this is that psychotherapy involves a relationship, but disabled people in institutions are perceived as people who need to be looked after or cared for in a depersonalised and ritualistic way and not related to as fellow human beings. This social defence system (Menzies-Lyth, 1959; Jaques, 1955) helps staff to cope with the intolerable anxiety of their task by avoiding guilt and uncertainty. The aim is a smooth-running social system. The cost is that staff, management and client are denied the possibility of rewarding interactions that reflect the reality of the chaos, sadness and ambivalence they all experience.

One aspect of the decision-making process that led to my working with Ron came paradoxically from the thinking behind the communicative approach (Holmes 1998; Langs, 1979), which is based on the therapist creating a holding therapeutic environment by setting up and managing a secure frame. The communicative approach views all people – clients and therapists alike – as potentially insightful and in possession of adaptive psychological resources. I believed that this strong democratic aspect of the approach would served as a safeguard and enable me to keep my respect for Ron, to address my shortcomings and any deviations, and to encourage both of us to trust his ability to find his own way.

LEARNING POINTS

- Contact with the client prior to the therapeutic relationship raises concerns for the psychodynamic therapist.
- The anonymity and some of the neutrality that are so important to the development of a secure therapeutic frame will be impaired if not completely absent.

IMPLICATIONS FOR THERAPISTS

The options open to a therapist who has known the client prior to the onset of counselling or therapy are to rule out the possibility of becoming the client's counsellor and to wait until a more neutral counsellor is found, or to risk the blurred boundaries that might occur in the case of impaired neutrality and anonymity.

Phase two: building trust

'Are you going to tell me off?' said Ron at the beginning of our first session. I replied, 'Although you have asked to see me for counselling, the fact that you also knew me as the manager here seems to cause confusion. You may be wondering whether I am really the counsellor or a manager in disguise?' Without hesitation Ron said 'Yes, I wanted counselling. Oh, how I miss my mother. My leg really hurts now. I think she put it in my leg. I did not think she would go when she did. There is only one person I like in the home – Linda. She is lovely. She is really nice to me. I like the dog, but Brenda thinks it is hers. I used to take the dog out with the wheelchair. I wish I had an electric wheelchair. They say that if I have an electric wheelchair I will never walk again. If my mother could see me now in a wheelchair she would have a fit.'

The fact that Ron had known me in my previous role as manager was obviously confusing his attempt to make sense of his world. Yet at the same time the familiarity could impart a sense of safety to the therapeutic relationship. Because of our shared past it is useful to consider the interplay between fantasy and reality as an aspect of transference. Transference is a displacement process that occurs in most therapeutic and other relationships. The therapist is invested with qualities, feeling and ideas that derive from the client's experiences outside therapy. Amongst the most common projections is that of authority and persecutory intentions. In this case, however, there was no need for displacement, the reality was that the therapist had actually been in an authoritarian position. 'Are you going to tell me off' could be read both as asking 'Do you still hold power over me?' and also as Ron telling me off for changing my identity and confusing matters. At one and the same time this confusion created hopes and caused disturbance. Like the mother who had died and left him, I had ceased to be the manager when I left the centre, but then I had come back in a different guise. Perhaps Ron thought that his mother might come back too. I was representing both the bad mother (manager) who had put the pain in his leg as well as Linda (counsellor) who was nice to him.

Forming an identity as a disabled man

For the first year of therapy Ron started almost every session with 'Am I in trouble again?' and 'Are you going to tell me off?' Not only did he not trust himself to be cared for by me, but he also was afraid, ready to be punished. He felt guilty, but guilty of what?

Melanie Klein (1940, p. 161) suggests that the death of a loved person, 'however shattering for other reasons, is to some extent also felt as a victory, and gives rise to triumph, and therefore all the more to guilt.' A sense of triumph was apparent in the joy Ron derived from disobeying his dead mother, as when he said 'My mother would have a fit if she could see me growing a beard.' Ron felt that his mother had not wanted him to grow up, to become a man. I believe his guilt stemmed from his Oedipal tendencies. The death of his father had frightened as well as delighted him. He said, 'Apart from helping to conceive me he did not do anything for me – and I am not sure there was not another man.' Could it be that in his omnipotence fantasy the other man was Ron himself, who had managed to get rid of this useless father and become his own father, and his mother's illicit partner? This takes us back to Ron allowing his left arm to be amputated at the age of 13. Why had he agreed to it? His declared reason was that others had made fun of his paralysed arm, but perhaps the amputation had in a bizarre way been a form of reparation. He had allowed a part of his body, an arm, to be cut off. The amputation of the arm, which symbolised masculinity and manhood (as in a weapon), could be seen as an offering in the form of symbolic castration, theraby alleviating his guilt for wishing to kill his father. Another reason could have been that the useless arm had symbolised his powerlessness over his body. Having it cut it off meant taking charge.

His father had not taught him anything, not even how to shave. This father had been a constant bad object who had confused Ron's view and experience of manhood. 'He worked very long hours and earned very little wages' – this was how Ron viewed his father's life, which had been about a great deal of hardship and very little gain. Yet the death of his father had enabled him to have his mother all to himself, which could have been the source of his Oedipal guilt. The experience of having his arm cut off and his father's death could have caused him to believe that the fate of useless objects, such as his paralysed arm and his poorly paid father, was to be cut off and forgotten. Such a belief would throw a terrifying light on his own predicament: he was endangered both by being a male, like his father, and by being disabled, like his arm. Perhaps the need to be taught how to shave, as well as being an initiation ritual into the male world was also about shaving off the beard as a sign of masculinity, in the same way as the arm had been shaved off as a phallic symbol.

However the main theme throughout our relationship was Ron's mother. In various ways Ron repeatedly said that when his mother died his world had fallen apart. Early on in therapy he said, 'You know they sent me a foster mother, but she was up to no good, I told her to go. You know that they think I set fire to my home after my mum died. I did do it but I did not do the second one. It was beautiful – the flames. I tried to stay in the fire but I could not. I wanted to die.'

It seems that Ron had never been able to achieve a mature separation from his mother. The message that he had received and internalised was that he was not a whole and autonomous person, so he could not and perhaps should not survive without his mother.

Soon after his mother died he had developed a fear of walking. He had been examined by a neurologist and a physiotherapist, neither of whom had been able find anything physically wrong with his legs. Ron had been afraid that if he fell there would be no one to pick him up. His fear had probably been due an inability to believe that he could stand up to the world alone, without his mother. His physical body had been expressing his emotional paralysis. As Margaret Mahler says of the child Teddy, 'He could walk, but he could not let go. He had to hold on. The child's ability to walk without holding on proves to the mother that he is growing up successfully and will be able to make it up in the big world. It seems as if the important autonomous function of free walking had become enmeshed in conflict' (Mahler *et al.*, 1975, p. 173). Teddy was only 15 months old while Ron was a 44 year old man, yet both shared the same phenomenon: they had the physical ability to walk but lacked the emotional ability to let go. Mahler sees the mother–child relationship as the major influence on the ability to walk freely, to move forward. When Ron's mother died he had lost the support he needed to stay upright. It seems that her death had returned him to being a toddler. When Ron talked about his inability to walk he said he was afraid of falling and being hurt. Perhaps because he had not managed to internalise his mother as his inner good object he was still dependent on her physical presence for support so was not ready to let go. Ron had not become an autonomous person and could not believe that it was possible to survive without his mother. He had not even been able to consider a substitute, as evidenced by his rejection of the foster mother.

I suggested to him that his wish to die might be a wish to be with his mother. Before I had finished his face lit up with a smile and he said, 'How did you know?' He was relieved to discover that he did not have to carry the burden of his secret alone, that it was possible to talk about his wish to be reunited with his mother.

There was another secret troubling Ron. About four months into therapy he blurted out, 'I found out that my parents were not married; it is terrible, why did they never tell me? My mother would kill me if she knew I told you about it.' The revelation of his parents' 'sin' became another theme in the therapy. Ron seemed to be very angry about it. He felt deceived. Was I also deceiving him? Was this connected to my change of role? In an attempt to understand what it was about I offered an interpretation: 'Perhaps you believe that your difficulties are in some way a result of your parents pretending to be married. Because they did not tell you, you could not prevent the troubles. You may also feel it is the same here; you don't know whether I am the manager or the counsellor.' Ron said, 'You are looking very tired, you know, the doctor who told my mum that I have to be in a wheelchair died. My mum and dad are dead. I don't know where it's all going to end, I want to kill myself.'

My interpretation was obviously not what he had wanted to hear. I had got it wrong, so I had become the bad mother who did not understand him and should be put to sleep. Ron was oscillating between the sense of power derived from his omnipotence fantasy and the anxiety brought about by attributing to himself the power to kill. He was telling me that the people who had been assigned to look after him were now dead. Was it an omnipotent warning that looking after him was dangerous, that if you failed him you would die?

I said, 'It seems to me that you are losing too many people and perhaps you are thinking there is something in you that causes them to die. The same thing that causes me to become tired.' He replied, 'The only good thing in the home is Lisa, the dog, but she is not really mine.' This time Ron felt heard, which brought Lisa to his mind. The dog had become the most important being in his life. She was invested with Ron's longings and emotions, as there was no one else who was able and willing to interact with him.

When I suggested that Lisa was a mother, Ron seemed pleased. He said 'Yes, how did you know? I use to hug and kiss her and call her "mummy". I want to kiss and cuddle Laurie [one of the residents in the home], but they say I should not.' The dog was providing the only closeness and warmth he had. The dog could be seen as a transitional object, as a bridge to the human contact he craved, but at present maturation and a real human relationship were being prevented by the institution and his lack of social skills.

One of his ongoing complaints against his mother was that 'She promised that I would go before her, that she would never leave me. I was there when she died. I did not let them take her. I did not believe she was dead.' Ron's world had been shattered and he felt cheated. Mother, the giver of life, had given up, had been defeated and lost her own life. It did not make sense. The deal he thought he had made by offering his arm as a sacrifice or a bribe had not been honoured.

The consequences of his mother's death were twofold: he had not been able to emerge from the symbiotic fusion with his mother, and he had never completed the separation individuation process. He still perceived himself as a part of the mother–Ron union, in which his mother held all the power and strength, such as the power to promise Ron that he would go before her, thus reversing the natural chronological order of death. The death of his mother had left him feeling exposed and vulnerable, bereft of his only close human contact. Although he had the ability, he had never acquired the necessary skills or experience to manage life in the world without the shield of his mother. He often recalled that after the operation on his brain at the age of 10 the doctor had told him that he would never learn to read or write. After saying this he usually told me the time: 'It is 1.32, we have only eighteen minutes left.' He was accurately reading the watch on my wrist, upside down, thereby challenging and mocking the judgment of the doctor and other professionals, me included.

What could be the reason for a man of 40 to be utterly dependent on his mother and fail to achieve full awareness of the self–other differentiation? Perhaps the message hidden in his mother's promise never to leave him was 'Because you cannot survive without me.'

Sarah was born with spina bifida. Throughout her childhood her mother kept telling her that she should have been born dead. This is an extreme example of a mother not trying to hide or contain her disappointment about giving birth to a disabled child and having no moral inhibitions about expressing her murderous wishes to the child. Unlike Sarah's mother, most parents manage to contain their negative feelings about their child's disability. In some cases this takes the form of reaction formation, which involves establishing an opposite pattern of behaviour and feelings in order to defend against intolerable and otherwise uncontrollable urges. An example of this is parents who overcompensate by totally devoting themselves to their disabled child. This type of over-care contains a wish to eliminate the impairment by 'loving the child to death'. However such devotion can smother the child, thus preventing any possibility of maturation. The parents create an environment in which the separation process cannot happen, so their disabled child will never become an autonomous adult. By overprotecting the child the parents are unconsciously responding to their need to reduce their guilt, thus minimising their 'unpleasure'. For parents who feel ashamed of having produced an impaired child, the provision of total care may be a way of burying their shame. It has to be said here that the attitude of parents of disabled children varies considerably, as all parent–child relationships.

LEARNING POINTS

- How is son made to believe that he cannot live without his mother?
- As we saw in previous chapter, some parents find it very difficult to cope with the fact that the child they have brought into the world is disabled. They constantly struggle with guilt and anxiety. Their feeling of guilt arises from their mixed reactions to having a disabled child. At one end of the scale is their sense of failure for not preventing the impairment. At the other end is their wish to obliterate the disability and sometimes the disabled child itself in order to hide their failure.

IMPLICATIONS FOR THERAPISTS

- Psychotherapists, especially those who work psychodynamically, may encounter within the client–therapist relationships characteristics that are similar in nature to 'total care' fusion, such as the temptation to turn the therapeutic dyad into a symbiotic, all-enveloping relationship.
- Therapists who offer open-ended therapy may sometimes seem to be saying, like Ron's mother, 'I will never leave you.'

■ As a basic precaution, therapists should be alert to the temptation to hide behind this all-powerful parental position.

Phase three: letting go

Ron's realisation that he was alone, without his mother, brought a strongly Kafkaesque note to his view of the world. His favourite phrases were 'I don't know where it is all going to end' and 'They want to get rid of me'. I believe that at times Ron saw me as part of 'they' and perhaps still linked me to my managerial role, especially when he asked 'Am I in trouble again?'

In a session preceding a two-week break Ron said, 'I like it very much being in a wheelchair. I like it best when I am pushed around.' I interpreted this as a reaction to my leaving him for two weeks, which may have made him feel that he could not trust people to be there for him and therefore the wheelchair was his only reliable source of support. When talking about being in the wheelchair Ron looked like a child talking about his favourite toy. The pleasure he expressed at being pushed around could be seen as connecting back to something that he associated with his mother; exchanging the possibility of autonomy and separation for the comfort of complete regression and enjoying the secondary gains of being disabled.

About a year into our therapeutic relationship Ron told me that he had become incontinent. He seemed embarrassed and asked, 'Do you mind me talking about it?' In my reply I linked the incontinence to his wish to be in a wheelchair, and suggested that he might also be wishing to become like a baby. Ron's response was very clear: 'I do not want to be a baby. I want to be a grown up man.' He was telling me off for infantilising him. His embarrassment indicated that inside the damaged and disfunctioning body there was someone who wanted to be treated as a sexually mature man.

Perhaps by acting like a baby and becoming unable to walk or control his bodily functions he was saying to his father and the therapist (onto whom was projected the paternal role): 'See what you have done to me. Father, you did not teach me how to stand up in the world and express my sexuality and be a man.' The therapist–father transference had been triggered by my interpretation, which conveyed that I, like all other carers, regarded him as a baby, as an asexual, undeveloped being.

Ron's incontinence was the last straw for the staff at the home in which he had resided since the death of his mother. They indicated that because of the deterioration of his physical ability, especially when combined with his awkward behaviour, he was now too much to cope with and there was talk of him being moved to another home.

For Ron this was a time of disturbing uncertainty as it brought back the experience of losing his first home when his mother died. During this period Ron resisted all interpretations that linked me to his mother: 'No, there is no other mother, and my mother is dead. You know I burnt the house after she died. They wanted to give me a foster mother but I did not like her. Now I am in a home, but they don't want me. They want to get rid of me. They are talking of another home. [Cheeky smile] I will burn the home.' Perhaps by warning me against making crass interpretations Ron was trying to protect me from the fate of his mother, thereby preventing yet another loss.

Ron's bewilderment and surprise began to turn into anger towards his mother. The very person he had believed would be there for him forever had rejected and abandoned him. Now it was happening all over again – the home that was suppose to act as a mother substitute was intending to do what his mother had done. Therefore he would punish it with fire, just as he had done to the home that had not kept his mother alive.

Ron continued, 'Laurie says that there is a devil in me. My mother knew there was a devil in me.' He was telling me that there was a dark and dangerous side to him. Perhaps he was attempting to find an answer to the question that has remained unanswered since asked by the Biblical Job: 'Why me?' In order to reduce his mental pain Ron created a split – it was not him who was being rejected and punished, it was the devil in him. It was the devil who had driven his mother away. When he had set the house on fire or was thinking of burning the home, Ron was punishing the devil by burning him at the stake. Failing to stay in the fire had made him realise that he could not separate himself from the devil, that burning the devil meant burning himself. The devil represented his aggression and his destructive fantasies, which he saw as endangering his loved ones. It followed that the people at the home would be willing to have him as long as they did not discover the devil in him. But his fellow resident Laurie had found out, and now they wanted to get rid of him before he destroyed them. Even Lisa the dog was not safe.

A few weeks later Ron came to see me in his new electric wheel-chair. He said, 'The other day I ran over the dog and the dog cried. It is strange to see animals cry. I asked her if she wanted me to rub her pain. I did and she perked up.' The electric wheelchair had become the embodiment of the destructive, omnipotent power of the devil. In an earlier stage of therapy he had called the dog 'mummy' and said he loved it more than anything else. Now the sense of power he had gained from his electric wheelchair enabled him to distance himself from the dog and objectify it. From being Lisa, his closest friend, it had become 'the dog', just an animal.

The process unfolding here had started when Ron invested the dog with the status of mother, which meant that the dog had occupied the highest position in Ron's internal emotional world. I would suggest that the dog–mother–lover link had been an attempt to adjust to life without the original mother by creating a safe and unthreatening substitute in the form of the dog, a transitional object. The dog was part of the home and had served as a means for Ron to feel a certain degree of relatedness to the home. The dog had provided enough closeness and connection for Ron to survive in what he saw as a strange and hostile environment. He had perceived the proposed change of home as confirmation of his 'badness'. He had been attacked from inside. The devil within him had caused him yet again to be punished and rejected. His attempt to connect to the good positive mother through Lisa, the dog, had failed. So Lisa had lost her special humanised status and was now nothing but a helpless animal.

Many disabled people experience the wheelchair as an extension of themselves. Possessing an electric wheelchair gave Ron an opportunity to externalise his sense of destructive power and control. This feeling of strength provided a temporary distraction from the internal devastation of being abandoned for the second time or, if his birth is counted the third time. The comparative freedom of movement and strength Ron derived from the power-driven instrument instilled in him a feeling of elation that helped to counteract his pain of rejection, for a while.

LEARNING POINT

■ Running over the dog could be seen as a symbolic act in which Ron was attempting to cut off the only emotional link he had with the home. By attacking this transitional object he may have been indicating that he had given up the struggle of finding a place in the world.

During the electric wheelchair phase Ron boasted, 'I bashed a gatepost yesterday and this morning I bashed into a wall here.' His time on the throne did not last long and a few weeks later he came in a manually operated chair. Ron explained,' 'They didn't allow me to bring my electric wheelchair, I don't know why. I like my electric wheelchair. I can go very fast. Sometimes I don't wait for the light when I cross the road.' Later in the session he said, 'You know what I want best? To be dead in a coffin so I could be with my mum.' The electric wheelchair was a weapon to destroy others, but it also offered the possibility of a 'ride to heaven'.

The loss of the electric wheelchair left Ron without a shell to protect him against the unknown and without a means of attacking the hostile world. Feeling defenceless because of the inevitability of his move it was time for stocktaking and counting past and future losses. In the session before his move to a new home he said, 'Lisa is lovely. I'll do my nut in if I lose Lisa. I like it in the home. The staff are going on courses. My mum is like my phantom fingers. They have been removed but I can still feel them.'

Ron was mapping out his world: the fingers on his amputated arm had gone, his mother was dead and he was about to lose his familiar residence. His lost love objects were turning into ghosts and phantoms that could haunt him, like his amputated fingers.

Autonomy and the institution

Moving to the new home brought with it many changes and made visible the limitations that institutions force on disabled people. One of those changes was that the centre where Ron's therapy took place was out of the new home's catchment area. Because of the experience I had had with the ways of local government I knew that without active negotiation with the new home it was highly likely that this would be the end of Ron's therapy. Yet again I found myself in a dilemma: on the one hand, as a representative of the counselling service I should try to arrange for the continuation of Ron's therapy. On the other hand I was his therapist, and therefore should remain neutral and refrain from involving myself in my client's affairs. This was one of those moments when the therapist is faced with a tussle between reality and the dictates of theory.

The issue at stake here was the client's autonomy. Autonomy, as discussed earlier, refers to the freedom to determine one's own actions and behaviour as a separate individual. Autonomy is not a fixed state of being; it is an ongoing process that depends on each individual's social, physical and emotional circumstances. Ron's circumstances had afforded him very little opportunity to develop his autonomy, and therapy gave him the only a space in which he could do so. Against the background of institutional life the importance of such space increases considerably.

IMPLICATIONS FOR THERAPISTS

Whose task is it to ensure that therapy is available to people such as Ron? The debate focuses on the following questions:

- Should a therapist take any practical steps to prevent further disabling by the system?
- To what extent would interaction with social workers and managers compromise the therapy?
- Is compromised therapy better than no therapy (bearing in mind that neutrality might be compromised from the beginning of therapy)?

In an ideal world the need for psychotherapy would be recognised by the system and appropriately provided for. In reality, however, the health and social support system finds it very difficult to recognise the need for psychotherapy, especially for disabled people. The latter's physical impairments often mask their emotional needs, so counselling or psychotherapy, if provided at all, tend to be abandoned in the face of the slightest complication. The provision of counselling and psychotherapy, when it exists, is very thinly structured. Often the therapist is the only professional, as in Ron's case, who is able and willing to fight for the continuation of the therapeutic work. However counsellors and therapists are trained to address the internal world of the individual; they are not trained to deal with institutions and the social system. Yet reality does impinge, and the therapist has to analyse the situation from three perspectives: the therapist's professional and theoretical convictions, the client's needs, and the system's support or resistance.

Because of Ron's isolation and lack of support outside the institution I decided to engage with his new home's management. The negotiations took sometime and about two months passed before counselling recommenced.

Soon after this long break Ron said, 'I am puzzled, can I come here? I do not know where it is all going to end. You know my electric wheelchair; it stopped in the middle of the road. I am confused; I don't know what to say. If my mum knew I was in a wheelchair she would have a fit.' I replied, 'You seem surprised. It is difficult for you to believe that you can come back here and see me every week. Perhaps that is why it feels as if every week you need to start it all over again.' Ron looked pleased and said 'True, I don't know, do you remember Lisa, the dog? I really miss her. There is no dog in the new place. I have lots of pain in my body. I am not with it. I don't really know what is going on. I am in my old place now.' Ron was talking about being confused, stuck and hopeless. The wheelchair stopping in the middle of the road could be seen as a metaphor for his body and his life. This instrument that was supposed to be supporting him had turned out to be unreliable and dangerous. I believe that despite the compromises involved, therapy provided Ron with the only continuity in his otherwise fragmented and uncontrollable world.

According to Hanna Segal, from birth the child is subject to conflict between the desire to annihilate the sudden change brought about by birth, including life itself, and the desire to live (see Miller, 1983). Ron had been subject to three sudden changes: his birth, the loss of his mother and family home, and then the loss of his first residential home. It seemed that in the battle between the desire to live and the wish to annihilate his own life, the latter was slowly gaining the upper hand.

Regression

Ron did not regain control over his body. He said, 'They are giving me pads now, so I will not wet myself. It never happened before. Who would believe that I would end up in a wheelchair? I was trying to kill myself, but I can't.' Since his move to the new home there had been a visible deterioration in his condition. I believe that his relationship with Lisa the dog had been the thin thread that held and fed his desire to live. In the past Ron had attempted to end his life in dramatic ways: in the house fire and in the wheelchair in the middle of the road. Having failed these attempts he had resorted to a slow regression towards the all-protecting womb/coffin by becoming more and more like a baby, which manifested itself in being incontinent and unable to walk.

Although the new home agreed to bring Ron for regular therapy, there were sometimes other calls for transport and it became difficult to keep to regular sessions. Ron now started each session by saying how hungry and thirsty he was. I made the obvious interpretation that because of the irregularity of our sessions he was not getting enough therapy or enough of me to satisfy his needs. It may have been an accurate interpretation, but it was not enough. Both Ron and I were out of control. I had become like his mother – promising to be there for him but unable to keep that promise.

When Ron arrived for the session that turned out to be our last his mouth was full of food, which he could neither chew nor swallow. It took a while before he was able to mumble 'Where can I throw it?' I put a paper napkin by his side and he spent the next 10 minutes fingering food out of his mouth and throwing it on the napkin on the floor. When his mouth was clear he said, 'Now I feel better, I would like to go home soon, but I don't know how I'll get back home, I am not sure. A few minutes later he said, 'I want to go to sleep.' He then fell asleep and slept for 23 minutes. It was a strange experience and I was not sure what was going on. What was he trying to express through the food and the sleep? Five minutes before the end of the session I became anxious and made a feeble intervention in order to wake him up. There was no response. Three minutes later he opened his eyes and looked at me. I said, 'You have been asleep; I just want to remind you that I will not be here next week. Do you want me to inform the home or shall I leave it to you?' To my surprise Ron responded in the clearest and most decisive way I had ever witnessed from him: 'I can deal with it, I have already told them.' As I was wheeling him out of the room his carer came along and said to me, 'Ron told us that you are not going to be here next week.' What had happened to the confusion and the 'I don't know'?

I never saw Ron again. He became unwell and died four weeks later.

Non-verbal communication

In that last session Ron provided a mostly non-verbal summary of his internal world. The food that stuck in his mouth was a metaphor for his position, stuck between life, which was symbolised by the wish to swallow and be nourished, and death, the wish to throw the food out and give up. He was not able to nurture or feed himself. Nor was anyone else, including those appointed to the task, such as his mother, the institutions and his therapist. He could not digest and internalise the care he was receiving; it was gagging him. Perhaps because I stayed with him when he was acting out his wish to give up and contained my disgust when he fingered the food out of his mouth, Ron felt accepted for what he was. He no longer seemed to be concerned about me, yet I believe that my presence was important in creating the space for growth that Winnicott (1958) describes as being alone with another.

Falling asleep in the session could be seen as a way of being with his dead mother. Also, being there while not being there, as in sleep, created a transitional space to move towards separation. According to Mahler *et al.* (1975, p. 29) infants' sleeping difficulties can be attributed to fear that their mother will disappear, so sound sleep is a first step towards separating from the mother.

Sleep is the ultimate relaxation. Only after throwing out the food and symbolically freeing himself of his internal debris was Ron able to let go and relax. Ron's falling asleep was like the infant who lets go and walks only when he has gained enough trust in both his ability to control and the holding environment. Ron's sleep was deep but controlled – he knew exactly when to wake up. In Winnicott's view:

> The state prior to that of aloneness is one of unaliveness, and the wish to be dead is commonly a disguised wish to be not yet alive. The experience of the first awakening gives the human individual the idea that there is a peaceful state of unaliveness that can be peacefully reached by an extreme of regression. (Winnicott, 1988, p. 132)

The transitional object

When I first met Ron he was in a transitional space, asking to leave one day-care institution and move back to the one he knew. Haunted by the ghost of his mother he was searching for familiarity and a sense of belonging.

Ron was on his way back, as if his life was a film being rewound. His transitional object, Lisa the dog, was used as part of this reversal. The idea of the transitional object, as developed by Winnicott, concerns the task of bridging the infant's journey from the purely subjective state of illusory omnipotence to a state of objective perception, making progress towards experiencing the external world as a separate individual. However for Ron the journey was one of regression into his inner world and away from external reality. The dog occupied the area between external reality and the dream or illusion of omnipotence. Harold Searles (1979) suggests that when a person who is still in a symbiotic state discovers that the relationship is under constant threat, an observer would realise with less surprise, as have many authors since Winnicott, that this or that particular element in the non-human environment is also experienced by the individual as a 'transitional object'; that is, it exists in the transitional domain between a reality that is not entirely internal and one that is not entirely external. Ron's experience of relating to others, including his therapist, was not providing sufficient input to promote the maturation needed to approach external reality.

Therapy in institutions

My decision to become Ron's counsellor was perhaps tinged with a fantasy of omnipotence and possibly some arrogance, such as presuming that there was nobody else who could do it, or that I would succeed against the odds. This decision took place in an institutionalised environment. Menzies-Lyth (1988) has made a major contribution to our understanding of the effect of institutions on both inmates and workers. Following Jaques (1955), she developed the idea of institutions as social defence systems, arguing that the role of the institution is to protect society from the anxiety provoked by the disturbing presence of disabled people.

Ron was brought up by a family that acted as an obedient agent of the social defence system – they protected society from his disturbing presence. By doing so they failed to facilitate the separation and individuation process during the early stages of his development. As a result, in adulthood Ron lacked the skills needed to function as an autonomous member of society. Would Ron have been treated in the same way if he had been a non-disabled person? Like most 'if' questions, we are not looking for a direct answer but another angle on the debate.

The rationale for deviating from the neutrality principal is that in a system that does not value psychotherapy for disabled people, sometimes therapy can only take place if the therapist takes action, thereby risking damaging some aspects of the therapeutic work. Unlike most adults, who are responsible for themselves, people in institutions are the responsibility of the institution. In the absence of anyone else to represent Ron it was left to me to approach the home's management in the initial stage of negotiating the therapeutic contract.

LEARNING POINT

- Against a background of confusion and uncertainty, offering consistency and reliability may be the only means of addressing the damage and creating an accepting environment in which it is possible to survive imperfection.

IMPLICATIONS FOR THERAPISTS

- Therapists who choose to work in an institution may at times be tempted to collude with the social defence system and find themselves torn between serving the defensive needs of the institution and facilitating clients' autonomy.
- It is therefore essential for them to have an adequate support system and regular supervision with an independent consultant,

thus creating a space for them to reflect upon their own reactions to institutional pressure.

■ Working in institutions requires therapists to have the flexibility to adapt their work to their clients' particular circumstances and to create a safe and stable space by maintaining clear boundaries.

Summary

Ron had never had the opportunity to develop an adult sense of reality. In our last session he communicated his wish to reach a peaceful state. His clarity and assertiveness was a triumph for him and a gift for me. It was as though he was saying, 'See, I am leaving proudly, with my dignity intact, I am in control, able to stand in the world and make a choice.' Ron chose to join his mother.

POSTSCRIPT

I had two aims in writing this book. The first was to explore the effects that disability has on non-disabled people, both as individuals and in the social context. Reported experiences of disabled and non-disabled people indicate that disability tends to trigger conscious or unconscious fear and anxiety, which often leads to overt or covert prejudices. Therefore a prerequisite for practitioners intending to work with disabled people is to identity and acknowledge their own defensive reactions to and prejudices about disability.

The second aim was to provide a model with which to approach relational and emotional issues that have a particular relevance to disability. The relational model of disability has proved to be a useful framework for the clinical practice taking place at SKYLARK – a counselling and psychotherapy agency for people affected by disability. I hope that other practitioners working with disabled people will find it helpful and will be able to incorporate some or all of the ideas into their practice.

Therapists and other caregivers who rely on verbal communication may benefit from recent developments in computer and communications technology, which offer new ways of interacting with speech-impaired individuals.

In the literature by and about disabled people, and in social and clinical interaction with disabled people, two main themes keep appearing: the challenge of developing intimate relationships, and the difficulty of making choices and controlling one's life. Therapists who want to gain an understanding of the significance and complexity of these themes need look no further than the parallel process of balancing trust and autonomy within the therapeutic relationship. Most people at times struggle to maintain this delicate balance, but for disabled people it is a particularly difficult challenge.

Trust is about willingness share aspects of one's inner world with another. When such sharing takes place in the therapeutic relationship it may at times be perceived as an invitation for fusion. Autonomy acts as a counterpoint, enhancing individuality and keeping separateness intact, thus preventing complete fusion.

When clients are frightened by painful and unpredictable events such as the onset of a chronic illness or the consequences of an accident, they may feel a desperate need to be looked after, to merge with a strong parental figure such as a therapist. At such times clients' tendency to relinquish responsibility may result in overdependency. This can be a trying time for therapists, who often choose this line of work because they want to help and be needed. They may find themselves torn between wanting to respond to the client's obvious wish for fusion and over-care on the one hand, and their awareness of the deceptive nature of such wishes on the other. However, even during what seems to be a regressive phase of therapy, maintaining clear boundaries provides the autonomous space needed for clients to develop trust in themselves and others.

Body image is often a problem for disabled people. Yet non-disabled writers and practitioners seem to be more concerned about the way impairment affects the body than are disabled people. Most of the clinical work and literature on this subject suggests that the infant initially perceives its impaired body as whole, that it is the nature of subsequent interactions, mainly the mother–baby relationship, and the social context that determine the individual's body image. However the data accumulated so far is not sufficient to support a conclusive view of this because it is anecdotal in nature and has not been backed by rigorous research. To broaden our understanding of the disabled person's formulation of body image we need to encourage inter-disciplinary discourse. For example the study of phylogenesis (the evolutionary development of a species through a succession of forms) offers a way of investigating how disabled group members perceive their 'form'. The issue to be explored is whether we all have an inherited unconscious blueprint of a whole body, regardless of the shape or state of the actual body, or whether the body image evolves through learning by comparison. Another area to be considered is neuroscientific research into the phantom limb, which grapples with the mystery behind the effect of amputation on body image. The relationship between the actual body and the internal or wished-for body needs further exploration.

I hope that the issues raised in this book and the relational model of disability used to explore them will encourage a much-needed dialogue on the discrepancy between the professional's view of disability and the felt experience of the disabled person, and will promote the inclusion and better understanding of disabled people.

BIBLIOGRAPHY

Affleck, G., McGrade, B. J., Allen, D. A. and McQueeny, M. (1985) 'Mothers' beliefs about behavioral causes for their developmentally disabled infant's condition: What do they signify?', *Journal of Pediatric Psychology*, **10**: 293–303.

Andersen, H. C. (1928) *Andersen's Fairy Tales*, London: John F. Shaw.

Babinski, J. (1917) *Hystere-pithiatism et Troubles Nerveux d'Ordre Reflexe: Syndrome Physiopathique*, Paris: Masson (English translation, Rolleston, University of London Press, 1918).

Baradon, T. (1991) 'Some thoughts on eccentricity and victimisation: a report on the treatment of a latency boy', *Journal of Child Psychotherapy*, **17**(1): 79–92.

Bateson, G. (1956) 'Towards a Theory of Schizophrenia', *Behavioral Science*, **1**: 251–64.

Bauby, J. (1997) *The Diving Bell and the Butterfly*, London: Fourth Estate.

Begum, N. (1996) 'Doctor, doctor . . . disabled women's experience of general practitioners' in J. Morris (ed.) *Encounters with Strangers*, London: Women's Press.

Bion, W. R. (1961) *Experiences in Groups*, London: Tavistock.

Bion, W. R. (1962) 'A theory of thinking', in *Second Thoughts*, London: Karnac.

Blackwell-Stratten, M., Bestin, M. L., Mayerson, A. B., and Baily, S. (1988) 'Smashin Icons', in M. Fine and A. Asch (eds), *Women with Disability: Essays in Psychology, Culture and Politics*, Philadelphia: Temple University Press.

Blos, P. (1967) 'The second individuation process of adolescence', *Psychoanalytic Study of the Child*, **22**: 162–86.

Bowlby, J. (1958) 'The nature of the child's tie to his mother', *International Journal of Psychoanalysis*, **39**: 350–73.

Brain, W. R. and Head H. (1941) 'Visual distortion with special reference to the regions of the right hemisphere', *Brain*, **64**: 244–72.

Brazelton, T., Koslowski, B. and Main, M. (1974) 'Origins of Reciprocity: Early Mother–Infant Interaction', in M. Lewis and L. Rosenblum (eds), *The Effect of the Infant on Its Caregiver*, London: Wiley, pp. 49–76.

Brown, C. (1954) *My Left Foot*, London: Minerva.

Buckley, P. (1986) 'Introduction', in P. Buckley (ed.), *Essential Papers on Object Relations*, New York: New York University Press, pp. xi–xxv.

Bullard, D. and Knight, S. (eds) (1981) *Sexuality and Physical Disability*, St. Louis: C.V. Mosby.

Cicerone, K. D. (1991) 'Psychotherapy after mild traumatic brain injury: relation to the nature and severity of subjective complaint', *Journal of Head Trauma Rehabilitation*, **6**(4): 30–4.

Clancier, A. and Kalmanovitch, J. (1984) *Winnicott and Paradox*, trans. A. Sheridan, London: Tavistock.

Crossley, R. and McDonald, A. (1984) *Annie's Coming Out*, Melbourne: Penguin.

Danseco, E. R. (1997) 'Parental beliefs on childhood disability: development insight on culture, child development and intervention', *International Journal of Disability, Development and Education*, **44**(1): 41–50.

Dartington, T. (1981) 'Authority and power', in E. Miller and E. Gwynne, *A Life Together*, London and New York: Tavistock, pp. 49–72.

Davis, A. (1989) *From Where I Sit*, London: Triangle.

Davis, R. and Wallbridge, D. (1981) *Boundary and Space*, Harmondsworth: Penguin.

De Bary, J. (1987) *Die Ersheimung des Symbiosm* (1879) in P. L. Giouvacchini, *A Narrative Textbook of Psychoanalysis*, London: Jason Aronson.

De Board, R. (1978) *The Psychoanalysis of Organisations*, London: Routledge.

Dembo, T., Leviton, G. L. and Wright, B. A. (1956) 'Adjustment to misfortune – a problem of social psychological rehabilitation', *Artificial Limbs*, **3**: 4–62.

Denmark, J. C. (1994) *Deafness and Mental Health*, London: Jessica Kingsley.

Dodds, (1951) *The Greeks and the Irrational*, Berkeley, CA: University of California Press.

Duff, K. (1993) *The Alchemy of Illness*, London: Virago.

Edgerton, R. B. (1981) 'Another look at culture and mental retardation', in M. J. Begab, H. C. Haywood and H. L. Garber (eds), *Psychological Influences in Retarded Performance: Vol. I. Issues and Theories in Development*, Baltimore, MD University Park Press, pp. 309–23.

Emanuel, R., Colloms, A., Mendelson, A., Muller, H. and Testa, R. (1990) 'Psychotherapy with hospitalised children with leukaemia: is it possible?', *Journal of Child Psychotherapy*, **16**(2): 21–36.

Erskine, A. and Judd, D. (eds) (1994) *The Imaginative Body*, London: Whurr.

Esten, G. and Willmott, L. (1993) 'Double bind messages: the effects of attitude towards disability on therapy', *Women & Therapy*, **14**(3/4): 29–41.

Fairbairn, W. R. D. (1952) *Psychoanalytic Studies of the Personality*, London: Routledge.

Fairbairn, W. R. D. (1954) 'Observation on the nature of hysterical states', *British Journal of Medical Psychology*, **27**: 105–25.

Ferenczi, S. (1999) 'Stages in the development of the sense of reality', in Julia Burosa (ed.), *Selected Writings* London: Penguin.

Finkelstein, V. (1980) *Attitudes and Disabled People: Issues for Discussion*, New York: World Rehabilitation Fund.

Freud, Anna (1967) 'Comments on trauma', in S. S. Furst (ed.), *Psychic Trauma*, New York: Basic Books.

Freud, S. (1900) *The Interpretation of Dreams*, Standard Edition, Vol. 4, Harmondsworth: Peguin, 1991.

Freud, S. (1905) *Three Essays on the Theory of Sexuality*, Standard Edition, vol. 7, Harmondsworth: Penguin.

Freud, S. (1911) *Papers on Technique*, Standard Edition, vol. 12, Harmondsworth: Penguin.

Freud, S. (1914) *Remembering, Repeating and Working Through*, Standard Edition, vol. 12, Harmondsworth: Penguin.

Freud, S. (1916) *Introductory Lectures on Psychoananlysis*, Standard Edition, vol. 15/16, Harmondsworth: Penguin.

Freud, S. (1917) *Mourning and Melancholia*, Standard Edition, vol. 14, Harmondsworth: Penguin.

Freud, S. (1920) *Beyond the Pleasure Principle*, Standard Edition, 18, Harmondsworth: Penguin.

Freud, S. (1923) *The Ego and the Id*, Standard Edition, vol. 14, Harmondsworth: Penguin.

Freud, S. (1924) *The Dissolution of the Oedipus Complex*, Standard Edition, vol. 14, Harmondsworth: Penguin.

Freud, S. (1925) *Inhibitions, Symptoms and Anxiety*, Standard Edition, vol. 20, Harmondsworth: Penguin.

Freud, S. (1930) *Civilization and its Discontent*, Standard Edition, 21, London. Hogarth Press:

Freud, S. (1973) *New Introductory Lectures on Psychoanalysis*, vols 1 and 2, Harmondsworth: Penguin.

Gerschick, T., and Miller, A. (1995) 'Coming to terms', in D. Sabo and D. Gordon (eds), *Men's Health and Illness*, London: Sage.

Giovacchini, P. L. (1987) *A Narrative Textbook of Psychoanalysis*, London: Jason Aronson.

Gluckman, C. (1991) 'The normal child with disabled parents: Mary', *Journal of Child Psychotherapy*, **17**(1): 95–106.

Graves, R. (1955) *The Greek Myths*, Baltimore, MD: Penguin.

Greeley, E. (1996) *The Unclear Path*, London: Hodder & Stoughton.

Greenacre, P. (1958) 'Early physical determination in the development of the sense of identity', *Journal of the American Psychoanalytic Association*, **6**: 612–27.

Greenberg, J. R. and Mitchell, S. A. (1983) *Object Relations in Psychoanalytic Theory*, Cambridge, Mass.: Harvard University Press.

Greenson, R. R. (1968) 'Dis-identifying from mother: its special importance for the boy', *International Journal of Psychoanalysis*, **49**: 370–4.

Grotstein, J. S. (1997) ' "Internal objects" or "chimerical monsters?": the demonic "third form" of the internal world', *Journal of Analytical Psychology*, **42**: 47–80.

Grzesiak, R. C. (1979) 'Psychological Services in Rehabilitation Medicine: Clinical Aspects of Rehabilitation Psychology', *Professional Psychology*, **10**: 511–20.

Guggenbühl-Craig, A. (1971) *Power in the Helping Professions*, Dallas, Tex.: Spring Publications.

Gunther, M. S. (1994) 'Countertransference issues in staff caregivers who work to rehabilitate catastrophic-injury survivors', *American Journal of Psychotherapy*, **48**: 208–20.

Guthrie, E. (1996) 'Emotional disorders in chronic illness: psychotherapeutic interventions', *British Journal of Psychiatry*, **168**: 265–73.

Hanbury, R. F. (1988) 'Competency: self-imposed professional discipline', *Medical Psychotherapy*, **1**: 207–9.

Harkness, S. and Super, C. (1994) 'The developmental niche: a theoretical framework for analysing', *Social Science and Medicine*, **38**: 217–26.

Harlow, H. (1979) *The Human Model: Primate Perspectives*, Washington, DC: Winston.

Hinshelwood, R. D. (1991) 'Psychodynamic formulation in assessment for psychotherapy', *British Journal of Psychotherapy*, **8**(2).

Holland, J. W. (1995) *A Doctor's Dilemma*, London: Free Association Books.

Holland, J. W. (1997) *Death Anxiety and Clinical Practice*, London: Karnac.

Holmes, C. A. V. (1991) 'The wounded healer', *Society for Psychoaanalytic Psychotherapy Bulletin*, **6**: 33–6.

Holmes, C. A. V. (1998) *There is No Such Thing as a Therapist*, London: Karnac.

Hume, D. (1977) *Enquiries*, Oxford: Clarendon Press.

Jaques, E. (1953) 'On the dynamics of social structure', *Human Relations*, **6**: 3–24.

Jaques, E. (1955) 'Social systems as a defence against persecutory and depressive anxiety', in Klein *et al.* (eds), pp. 497–98.

Jureidini, J. (1988) 'Psychotherapeutic implications of severe physical disability', *American Journal of Psychotherapy*, **42**: 297–307.

Kohut, H. (1977) *The Restoration of the Self*, New York: International University Press.

Keith L. (1994) *Mustn't Grumble: Writing by Disabled Women*, London: Women's Press.

Keith, L. (2001) *Take Up Thy Bed and Walk*, London: The Womens Press.

Kernberg, O. F. (1995) *Love, Relations, Normality and Pathology*, New Haven, CT: Yale University

Kirk, G. S. and Raven, J. E. *The Presocratic Philosophers*, London: Cambridge University Press.

Klein, M. (1932) *The Psychoanalysis of Children*, London: Hogarth Press.

Klein, M. (1940) 'Mourning and its relation to manic-depressive state', *International Journal of Psychoanalysis*, **Xxi**: 125–53.

Klein, M. (1948) *Contributions to psychoanalysis*, London: Hogarth Press.

Klein, M. (1952) 'The origins of transference', *International Journal of Psychoanalysis*, **XXXIII**.

Klein, M. (1975) *Envy and Gratitude and other works: 1946–1963*, London: Hogarth Press.

Klein, M. (1946) *Notes on Some Schizoid Mechanisms: Envy and Gratit other Works*, New York: Delacote Press.

Kohut, H. (1978) 'Forms and transformation of narcissism', in P. Orienstein (ed.), *The Search for the Self*, vol. 1, New York: International University Press.

Kohut, H. (1984) *How Does Analysis Cure?* Chicago: University of Chicago Press.

Kraemer, S. (1994) 'The body goes mad: hospital liaison psychiatry in sickle-cell disease', in A. Erskin and D. Judd (eds), *The Imaginative Body*, London: Whurr, pp. 200–21.

Laing, R. D. (1961) *Self and Others*, London: Penguin.

Langs, R. (1979) *The Therapeutic Environment*, New York: Jason Aronson.

Langs, R. (1988) *A Primer of Psychotherapy*, New York: Garden Press.

Langs, R. (1992a) *A Clinical Workbook for Psychotherapists*, London: Karnac.

Langs, R. (1992b) *Science, Systems and Psychoanalysis*, London: Karnac.

Langs, R. (1997) *Death Anxiety and Clinical Practice*, London: Karnac.

Laplanche, J. and Pontalis, J.-B. (1973) *The Language of Psychoanalysis*, London: Karnac.

Leonard, C. J. (1985) 'Brief outlines of the parent/family reaction to childhood disability in families from three ethnic minority groups', *International Journal for Advancement in Counselling*, **8**, pp. 197–205.

Lewis, L. and Langer, K. G. (1994) 'Symbolization in psychotherapy with patients who are disabled', *Journal of Psychotherapy*, **48**: 231–9.

Lichtenstein, H. (1961) *The Dilemma of Human Identity*, New York: Jason Aronson.

Liedloff, J. (1975) *The Continuum Concept*, Harmondsworth: Penguin.

Lowe, G. R. (1972) *The Growth of Personality*, Harmondsworth: Penguin.

Lussier, A. (1960) 'The analysis of a boy with congenital deformity', *Psychoanalytic Study of the Child*, **15**: 430–53.

Lussier, A. (1980) 'The physical handicap and the body ego', *International Journal of Psychoanalysis*, **61**: 179–85.

Mahler, M. (1965) On the significance of the normal separation individuation phase', in M. Schur and A. Solnit (eds), *Drives, Affects, Behaviour*, vol. 2, New York: International University Press.

Mahler, M. (1968) *On Human Symbiosis and the Vicissitudes of Individuation, vol. 1. Infantile Psychosis*, New York: International University Press.

Mahler, M. S., Pine F. and Bergman, A. (1975) *The Psychological Birth of the Human Infant*, London: Karnac.

Marks, D. (1999) *Disability*, London: Routledge.

Marmor, J. (1953) 'An occupational hazard in the practice of psychotherapy', *The Journal of the American Psychiatric Association*, **110**: 370–6.

Masson, J. (1990) *Final Analysis*, London: Fontana.

McDougall, J. (1989) *Theatres of the Body*, London: Free Association

Menzies-Lyth, I. (1959) 'The function of a social system as a defence against anxiety: a report on a study of the nursing service of a general hospital', *Human Relations*, **13**: 95–121.

Menzies-Lyth, I. (1988) *Containing Anxiety in Institutions*, London: Free Association Books.

Merleau-Ponty, M. (1962) *Phenomonology of Perception*, London: Routledge.

Miller, E. and Gwynne, G. (1972) *A Life Apart*, London: Tavistock.

Miller, J. (1983) *States of Mind*, New York: Methuen.

Milner, M. (1950) *On Not Being Able to Paint*, London: Heinemann.

Morris, J. (1989) *Able Lives*, London: Women's Press.

Morris J. (1991) *Pride Against Prejudice: Transforming Attitudes Towards Disability*, London: Women's Press.

Morris, J. (1996) *Encounter with Strangers: Feminism and Disability*, London: Women's Press.

Murphy, R. (1990) *The Body Silent*, New York: W. W. Norton.

Nagera, H. (ed.) (1981) *Basic Psychoanalytical Concepts on the Libido Theory*, London: Karnac.

Nichols, K. A. (1984) *Psychological Care in Physical Illness*, London: Chapman & Hall.

Nolan, C. (1988) *Under the Eye of the Clock*, London: Pan.

Oliver, M. (1990) *The Politics of Disablement*, London: Macmillan.

Oliver, M. (1996) *Understanding Disability: From Theory to Practice*, London: Macmillan.

Olkin, R. (1999) *What Psychotherapists Should Know about Disability*, New York: Guilford Press.

Penfield, W. and Rasmussen, T. (1950) *The Cerebral Cortex of Man: A Clinical Study of Localisation of Function*, New York: Macmillan.

Perot, P. (1963) 'The brain's record of auditory and visual experience', *Brain*, **86**: 595–696.

Piaget, (1977) 'Equilibration processes in the psychobiological development of the child', in H. E. Gruber and J. J. Voneche (eds), *The Essential Piaget*, New York: Basic Books, pp. 832–41.

Piccioli, E. (1997) 'Interview with John Gedo', *The psychoanalytic Review*, **84**(1): 1–15.

Quadrio, C. (1992) 'Sex and gender and the impaired therapist', *Australian and New Zealand Journal of Psychiatry*, **26**: 346–63.

Ramachandran, V. S. and Blakeslee, S. (1998) *Phantoms in the Brain*, New York: William Morrow.

Richard, C. (1965) *Climbing Blind*, London: Hodder & Stoughton.

Reinhart, M. (1989) *Chiron and the Healing Journey*, London: Arkana.

Reiter, S., Mar'i, S. and Rosenberg, Y. (1986) 'Parental attitudes toward the developmentally disabled among Arab communities in Israel: a cross-cultural study', *International Journal for Rehabilitation Research*, **9**: 355–62.

Riviere, J. (1952) 'General introduction' in Klein *et al.*, *Developments in Psychoanalysis*, London: Hogarth.

Robertson, J. (1953) (film) *A Two-Year-Old Goes to Hospital*, New York University Film Library.

Rycroft, C. (1968) *A Critical Dictionary of Psychoanalysis*, London: Penguin.

Sacks, O. (1984) *A Leg to Stand On*, London: Picador.

Sacks, O. (1989) *Seeing Voices*, London: Pan.

Searles, H. F. (1959) 'Integration and deferentiation in schizophrenia', *Journal of Nervous and Mental Disease*, **129**: 542–50.

Searles, H. F. (1965) *Collected Papers on Schizophrenia and Related Subjects*, London and New York: Hogarth.

Searles, H. F. (1973) 'Concerning therapeutic symbiosis', *Annual of Psychoanalysis*, **1**: 251–2.

Searles, H. F. (1979) 'Counter-transference, a related subject', *Selected Papers*, New York: International University Press.

Segal, H. (1975) 'Notes on symbol formation', *International Journal of Psychoanalysis*, **38**: 391–7.

Segal, H. (1986) *Introduction to the Work of Melanie Klein*, London: Hogarth Press and Institute of Psycho-Analysis.

Seligman, M. E. P. (1975) *Helplessness*, New York: W. H. Freeman.

Shakespeare, T. (1998) *The Disability Studies Reader: Social Science Perspective*, Selig London: Cassell.

Shakespeare, T., Gillespie-Sells, K. and Davies, D. (1996) *The Sexual Politics of Disability*, London: Cassell.

Sinason, V. (1992) *Mental Handicap and the Human Condition*, London: Free Association Books.

Smith, D. L. (1991) *Hidden Conversation*, London: Routledge.

Sperber, H. (1912) 'Uber den Einfluss sexueller Momente auf Entstehung und Entwicklung der Sprache', *Imago, I*, 405.

Stern, D. (1985) *The Interpersonal World of the Infant*, London: Karnac.

Stoller, R. J. (1985) *Presentation of Gender*, New Haven, CT: Yale University Press.

Storr, A. (1972) *Human Destructiveness*, London: Routledge.

Storr, A. (1997) *Solitude: A Return to the Self*, London: HarperCollins.

Sutton, A. (1991) 'Depravation entangled and disentangled', *Journal of Child Psychotherapy*, **17**(1): 61–76.

Swart, G. T. (1991) 'An unusual approach to psychotherapy', *Canadian Journal of Psychiatry*, **36**(6): 467.

Taylor, G. J. (1987) *Psychodynamic Medicine and Contemporary Psychoanalysis*, Madison, CT: International Universities Press.

Taylor, G. J. (1994) 'The psychotherapeutic application of a dysregulation model of illness', in A. Erskin and D. Judd (eds.) *The Imaginative Body*, London: Whurr.

Thomas, K. (1971) *Religion and the Decline of Magic*, London: Penguin.

Thomas, R. K. and Garske, G. (1995) 'Object relations theory: implications for the personality development and treatment of persons with disabilities', *Journal of Melanie Klein and Object Relations*, **13**: 31–63.

Threvarthen, C. (1985) 'Facial expressions of emotion in mother–infant interaction', *Human Neurology*, **4**:

Tyson, P. and Tyson, R. L. (1990) *Psychoanalytic Theories of Development*, Yale University Press

Viinamaki, H., Kuikka, J., Tiihonen, J. and Lehotonen, J. (1998) 'Change in monoamine transporter density related to clinical recovery: a case-control study', *Nordic Journal of Psychiatry*, **52**: 39–44.

Warr, P. (1971) 'Employee well-being', in P. Warr (ed.), *Psychology at Work*, London: Penguin.

Weiss, M. (1997) 'Territorial isolation and physical deformity: Israeli parents' reaction to disabled children', *Disability & Society*, **12**(2): 259–71.

Williams, D. (1992) *Nobody Nowhere*, London: Bantam.

Williams, D. (1994) *Somebody Somewhere*, London: Bantam.

Winkley, L. (1990) 'Living with chronic illness: consultation to a children's renal dialysis unit', *Journal of Child Psychotherapy*, **16**(2): 49–62.

Winnicott, D. W. (1955) 'Metapsychological and clinical aspects of regression within the psychoanalytical set-up', *International Journal of Psychoanalysis*, **36**: 16–26.

Winnicott, D. W. (1964) *The Child, the Family, and the Outside World*, London: Pelican.

Winnicott, D. W. (1965a) 'The theory of parents–infant relationship', in *The Maturational Process and the Facilitating Environment*, New York: International Universities Press.

Winnicott, D. W. (1965b) *The Family and Individual Development*, London: Tavistock.

Winnicott, D. W. (1971) *Playing and Reality*, Harmonds worth: Penguin.

Winnicott, D. W. (1975a) 'Hate in the countertransferance', in *Through Paediatrics to Psychoanalysis*, London: Hogarth Press.

Winnicott D. W. (1975b) 'Paediatrics and psychiatry', in *Through Paediatrics to Psychoanalysis*, London: Hogarth Press.

Winnicott, D. W. (1975c) 'Transitional analysis objects and transitional phenomena, in *Through Paediatrics to Psychoanalysis*, London: Hogath Press.

Winnicott, D. W. (1986) *Home is Where We Start From*, Harmonds worth: Penguin.

Winnicott, D. W. (1988) *Human Nature*, London: Free Association Books.

Wyndham, J. (1979) *The Chrysalids*, London: Penguin.

Young, R. M. (1994) *Mental Space*, London: Process Press.

INDEX